Integr@ting
Technology
IN LEARNING
& TEACHING

PAT MAIER

ADAM WARREN

Integr@ting Technology

IN LEARNING

& TEACHING

a practical
guide for
educators

KOGAN
PAGE

First published in 2000

Kogan Page Limited
120 Pentonville Road
London N1 9JN
UK

Stylus Publishing Inc.
22883 Quicksilver Drive
Sterling, VA 20166-2012
USA

British Library Cataloguing in Publication Data

A CIP record for this book is available from the British Library.

ISBN 0 7494 3180 6

Typeset by Jean Cussons Typesetting, Diss, Norfolk
Printed and bound in Great Britain by Thanet Press Ltd, Margate

Contents

Contents

Introduction

This book has been written in response to our own need for a resource book for academics engaging in communication and information technologies (C&IT) learning and teaching innovations, whether working independently or within designated courses. There is a wealth of literature in the sector and on the Web around this topic, but it tends to be dispersed and not necessarily placed within the working agendas of most academics or within an integrated educational framework. While realizing that we have not managed to cover everything we wished to in the book, we have attempted to provide this framework for practitioners by discussing the:

- 'political' agendas that are driving this forward, as well as the UK support mechanisms that have been put in place to help this happen;
- pedagogical framework of open and independent learning that can be enabled by the use of C&IT;
- technical issues surrounding the production and delivery of digital learning materials.

Who is this book for?

This is an ideal resource for academics/educators who are using, or contemplating using, C&IT in their teaching. It looks at wider educational issues and discusses where C&IT can be used most effectively. There are a variety of reflective activities throughout the book that encourage readers to consider their position with regard to the issues. Each chapter (except Chapter 1) has a checklist that serves to conclude the chapter. For more experienced users of C&IT, these checklists can be read first, allowing readers to pick up on certain issues without having to read the whole chapter.

This book is also an ideal resource or course book for educational developers devising staff development programmes concerned with these issues. The reflective exercises can be further developed for workshops.

Overview

Chapter 1 looks at the social agendas influencing the changes we are experiencing in higher education today in order to illustrate that we are currently moving through a revolutionary period. Whether we accept these changes is not the issue: the fact is that change is occurring faster than at any time most of us can remember. An essential part of this change is the application of C&IT to our everyday lives. This chapter also expands on the UK support that is available to those wishing to take advantage of it.

Chapter 2 discusses the move to resource-based learning as a form of open, independent learning. It looks at what it means to be an independent learner and ways of supporting this, together with issues of student accessibility when devising electronic resource bases. It also discusses how our teaching resources can be digitized and become learning resources that can be used in networked learning environments.

Chapter 3 discusses the kind of learning activities best suited to independent or autonomous learning – activities that encourage collaborative work and critical thinking. These can range from full open learning packages to experimentation with innovative group ideas. The chapter continues by discussing design strategies for open learning via electronic resource-based learning.

Chapter 4 considers computer-mediated communication and its role in group learning. It investigates the use of technology to facilitate discussion, collaborative work and peer-assisted learning and presents guidelines on setting up and managing such activities. It concludes by outlining the other ways in which online communications can support learning and teaching and reviews the technologies available.

Chapter 5 looks at assessment and in particular the development of learning outcomes and assessment criteria. It considers the general application of technology to this field and how to create good multiple-choice questions that tap into critical thinking.

The Active*Guide Web site

Reference is made throughout the book to a complementary Web site, called the Active*Guide. This is available at http://www.clt.soton.ac.uk/activeguide. You will need to enter a username and password each time you access the Active*Guide:

username: active
password: guidance

Please do not publish these details in print, on the Web or via e-mail lists. Thank you.

This Web site will maintain an up-to-date list of all the Web references in the book as well as further links to relevant resources as we find them. It will also provide additional information to supplement that printed in the book:

Tools of the Trade discusses the specific software systems that are available and, since it is on a Web site, these will be updated as technology changes.

Try Something Simple will be a set of learning materials that will guide you through the use of some of the technology. We realize there is a learning curve for this and recommend that you start modestly, building your confidence in using the technology both pedagogically and technically.

We would like you to see this book and its Web site as a resource that helps you explore these aspects of learning and teaching, and that hopefully resonates with your institution's own learning and teaching strategy.

1

Agendas for change in higher education

In this chapter we discuss the wider agendas affecting the many changes that are happening in higher education on a global scale. All countries are now faced with a reassessment of how higher education should be delivered to meet the needs of a changing economic order that will demand:

- more skilled workers (so called *knowledge workers*);
- more flexibility and therefore *lifelong learning* skills;
- more 'self starters' in a more autonomous and team-spirited working environment (*independent learning* and *key skills*).

All of this results in a mass higher education system that is reassessing its learning and teaching practices and exploiting the use of communication and information technologies (C&IT) to serve the sector. Some of these experiences are reflected in the following external pressures:

- audits on teaching quality, research and employability (quality assurance);
- increased need for staff and students to be C&IT literate;
- insufficient library resources (reduction of unit funding);
- reduced departmental resources (more students, less staff);
- more diverse student body (widening participation);
- industry's demand for key skills (partnerships with 'industry'/lifelong learning).

These lead to:

- an increased awareness of *how* we teach (more learner centred);
- flexible provision of learning resources for open learning;
- an introduction of collaborative learning (student autonomy);
- encouraging reflective practice for a culture of lifelong learning;
- integrating key skills into the curriculum.

This chapter will contextualize these changes, looking at the various agendas that are impacting on us in higher education. Hopefully, this chapter will show that these changes are not just an educational whim or another hoop we have to jump through.

The changes we are feeling are global and our colleagues in most other countries are experiencing similar frustrations, or excitement.

1.1 The 'political' agenda

The 'political' or 'external' agenda is bombarding us from a variety of sources, including changes in society, from the so-called 'information revolution' to issues of quality and accountability for our teaching, both individually and institutionally. In addition to this, we are seeing an increasing professionalization of lecturers as educators. We are living through a major revolution in the provision of higher education and having to adapt simultaneously to challenges on all fronts: we are becoming 'change weary'. However, adapt we must, and if we see it as part of our own 'lifelong learning' then maybe we can rise to the occasion and enjoy it.

1.1.1 The impact of the information revolution on higher education

The *information revolution* is linked with the *knowledge economy* and *globalization*. These movements are pointing the way to a new economic and social order. These changes have rapidly expanded since the fall of Communism (Lubbers, 1999a). Technology has been one of the prime movers, not only affecting the economic order but also political and cultural spheres (Lubbers, 1999b).

The knowledge economy

OECD economies are placing increasing emphasis on the production, distribution and use of knowledge in industries such as computers, electronics and aerospace, which are being supported by knowledge-intensive sectors such as education, communications and information. This *knowledge economy* is dependent on people's ability to adapt to new situations, update their knowledge, know where to find knowledge (networking), and to apply it to new situations. These are so-called *knowledge workers*, being paid for their knowledge skills rather than manual work. OECD (1996) estimates that more than 50 per cent of the gross domestic product in the main OECD economies is now in knowledge-based activities. The education sector across OECD countries is expanding to meet the need to provide this highly skilled labour force. In addition to 'information', some of the new skills that are prized are flexibility, initiative, creativity, problem solving and openness to change – basically, employers are looking for the lifelong learner with a good set of key skills.

The pressures we are feeling in higher education are originating primarily from the need to meet the demands of this new economic order. The UK government target is for one-third of young people to attend higher education, which according to the Report of the National Committee of Inquiry into Higher Education (NCIHE, 1997) chaired by Sir Ron Dearing, has been largely met. However, although spending on education has increased in the UK, there has been a reduction of 40 per cent in the amount spent per student. So, we are recruiting more students and feeling the pressures of decreased unit funding, while according to OECD (1997), only approximately 30 per cent (in the UK, Australia, Canada and the US together) of a typical cohort on a four-year or less programme will complete. However, a report from the Higher Education Funding Council for England (HEFCE, 1999) showed that in England only 18 per cent of full-time undergraduates fail to complete their studies compared with 45 per cent in France and 28 per cent in Germany. So there is a wide variation between OECD countries.

Globalization of higher education

Globalization is another factor emerging within the knowledge economy, which has been led by an increasing awareness of interdependence in world affairs, and partly attributed to advances in communications and information technology. Another main factor concerns the ideology of 'free trade' that has diminished country boundaries and merged economic interdependence. Global enterprises are themselves more network-oriented, having a flat organizational structure with increasing autonomy on the shop floor (Lubbers,1999a), reinforcing the need for those who are self-starters and team-workers.

The Internet can bring us into immediate contact with someone almost anywhere in the world and allow us to gain access to information that in the past would have taken weeks, if not months, to find. We can send completed work across the world in minutes. This almost instant access to our global partners and information has reduced 'geography' on a scale not seen before. Globalization in higher education is more than 'very distant' learning courses: it is a change in mindset where it is likely to be multiple, interdependent centres instead of one – ie, cooperation between institutions which are flexible and encourage the propagation of international perspectives.

At present there is not much evidence of real globalization in education taking place, although we are seeing an emerging sector. In the US, Western University has 15,000 students across 64 locations. California Virtual University and the Southern Regional Electronic Campus are similarly large networked organizations offering hundreds of courses. Sylvan Learning Systems, originally an educational testing company, now has links with the Massachusetts Institute of Technology and University of Technology at Berkeley with 48 sites in shopping malls and business centres (cited in Thorne, 1999). Educational companies such as these will become more consumer-oriented, offering qualifications (products) in an ever more competitive market where they will need to be flexible to meet the changing demands of society and the availability of their students.

Time Warner and Microsoft, for example, are also exploring links with certain US research-led universities. This combination links the technological delivery medium with the content. Research has seen this globalization taking place for quite a while now with increasing numbers of international projects, linked through the UK Joint Academic Network (JANET), that allows academics to communicate over the Internet. Traditional universities are not this flexible and are not consumer-oriented, but once governments free up the monopoly of the universities to offer higher educational qualifications, we may see more mergers with other educational providers. Michael Thorne, vice-principal at Napier University in Scotland, claims that governments should allow universities to operate as publicly traded companies in order to meet these demands. New Zealand already has a framework in place where companies can award their own degrees and this is likely to be an expanding area in the future (cited in Thorne, 1999).

The language of dominance for the current wave of globalization is English, and on the negative side this produces a very monocultural approach to education. It is vital, therefore, that globalization leads to *global* interaction and not a cultural dominance. One of the criticisms of globalization is that it is dominated by an American ideology. It should be the role of global education to counterbalance the views of any dominant group, thus making it much more multi-perspective than before.

Qualifications themselves are also being set within a wider international context, thus paving the way for globalization. The UK Quality Assurance Agency, for example, has just set out a new National Qualifications Framework that aims to make qualifications transparent nationally and internationally. The basic component for this is the 'credit' system, where courses at particular levels within higher education will be standardized in terms of complexity, degree of student autonomy and the number of learning hours necessary. This restructuring of higher education is happening in many parts of the world, and in Europe it has been reinforced by the 1998 Sorbonne and the 1999 Bologna declarations, which aim to establish standardization of qualifications and promote student mobility.

The principal technology that has made global education viable, and therefore virtual universities possible, is the World Wide Web. This technology offers an integrated global environment for both resources and communications (synchronous – an analogy being the 'telephone', and asynchronous – an analogy being the 'letter'), and it is already being used increasingly for traditional full-time students.

Since education is one of the service growth areas for the knowledge economy, and globalization is an expanding phenomenon at political, economic, technological and cultural levels (Lubbers, 1999b), then the globalization of education is merely a matter of time. There needs to be a significant change in the mindset of politicians, educators and students. Procedures that ensure standards and quality must be established, and structures need to be put in place to make it a practical option for students.

Globalization Studies Web site

http://www.globalize.org/index.html

This site is a resource, an archive and a forum for students and educators interested in the process and consequences of globalization. The site was founded by Ruud Lubbers, professor of globalization and former Prime Minister of The Netherlands. This site offers a range of links and publications on the wide-ranging topic of globalization.

Virtual University Association

http://www.virtualuniversity.com/default.html

This is a network for those interested in virtual universities who aim to keep their members informed about technological changes that directly affect distance learning.

Virtual University Journal

http://www.openhouse.org.uk/virtual-university-press/vuj/archive.htm

This is a refereed international journal focusing on lifelong learning. You are able to see the title of the papers on offer but you cannot access them unless you subscribe. For an individual it currently costs £50 per year.

Department for Education and Employment: The Learning Age

http://www.lifelonglearning.co.uk/response/index.htm

A wide variety of information on several aspects of the 'learning age'.

Quality Assurance Agency for Higher Education

http://www.qaa.ac.uk/NQF/Overview.htm

The discussion document on the UK National Qualifications Framework.

1.1.2 Reforms in UK higher education

The knowledge economy and globalization can be seen as catalysts for change in education throughout society. A simplified view is shown in Figure 1.1.

Here we will only consider higher education and the impact of the Dearing Report (for England, Wales and Northern Ireland) and Garrick Report (for Scotland) on the process of reform. These reports were commissioned by the UK government to look into the future of higher education, and they have been marker documents for many of the developments in UK higher education that have followed since their publication in 1997. Some examples from the NCIHE 'Dearing Report' are:

- the implementation of learning and teaching strategies within all higher education institutions (recommendation 8);
- widening participation (recommendation 5, 6);
- staff to receive appropriate training to exploit uses of C&IT (recommendation 9);
- lifelong learning (recommendation 11);
- embedding of key skills in the curriculum (recommendation 17, 20, 21);
- benchmarks for degree standards (recommendation 25);
- professionalization of teaching within higher education through the Institute for Learning and Teaching (recommendation 14, 48).

Changes in approach to higher education

The most characteristic change in approach was signalled by a shift from 'teaching and learning' to 'learning and teaching' that first appeared in the Dearing Report. This linguistic shift signals the emphasis on learning as opposed to teaching, with study programmes being specified in terms of *learning outcomes* instead of teaching objectives. Learning and teaching strategies (recommendation 8) are now developed that similarly emphasize this change, and lecturers are seen as facilitators of student learning, developing approaches that encourage students to reflect on their progress. Most higher education institution (and departmental) learning and teaching strategies are therefore developed with a philosophy to encompass this. Lifelong learning, and its supporting

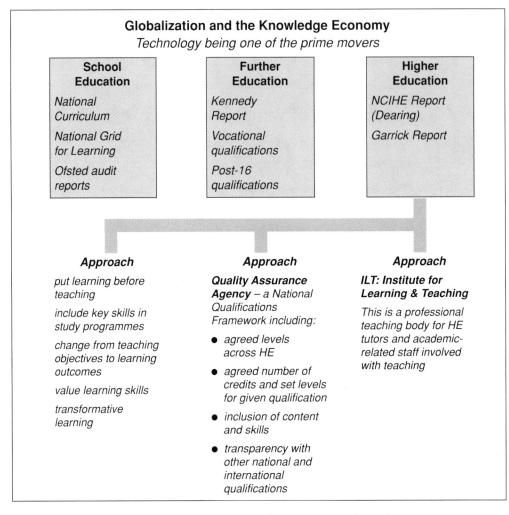

Figure 1.1 *Contextual perspective for the reforms in UK higher education*

concept – *independent learning* together with *widening participation* – are some of the key changes we are currently facing in higher education today.

📖 Department for Education and Employment: Lifelong Learning

http://www.lifelonglearning.co.uk/

This site contains a series of pages and papers on issues around lifelong learning.

📖 Widening Participation in Higher Education

http://wwwd2.leeds.ac.uk/ncihe/nr_101.htm

This is Chapter 7 of the NCIHE Report.

Standards

Recommendation 25 of the Dearing Report was directed to the UK Quality Assurance Agency (QAA) to set up a qualifications framework that would meet the needs of both academic and vocational learning. This qualifications framework has set standards within higher education. In England, Wales and Northern Ireland, for example, there are now five levels: HE5 doctorate, HE4 masters, HE3 bachelor degrees with honours, HE2 higher education diploma and HE1 higher education certificate. These levels have descriptors that indicate their level of difficulty in terms of complexity and autonomy required by the learner. This will be achieved across subject levels (approximately 40 subjects in total) through benchmark standards, which will contextualize generic learning domains such as general intellectual skills and attributes, subject-related knowledge, understanding and skills, and personal independence and responsibility. Independent learning, key skills and lifelong learning skills are therefore being built into study programme standards, against which we will be held accountable.

Both the Dearing Report and the QAA level descriptors indicate the type of learning that is to take place on study programmes. It is interesting to map these to the OECD's view of knowledge for a knowledge society, as shown in Table 1.1. Economists have codified the type of knowledge they feel is necessary for the success of such an economy, using this as a tool for economic analysis.

Table 1.1

OECD Knowledge Codification	'Dearing' Categories of Intended Learning Outcomes	QAA Level Descriptors
Know-what – facts, information	**Knowledge and understanding**	**Subject-related knowledge**
Know-why – scientific knowledge, principles, laws, concepts, theories	**Cognitive skills** – understanding methodologies and an ability for critical analysis	**General intellectual attributes**
Know-how – skills & capability to do something/select relevant & disregard irrelevant information	**Subject-specific skills**	**Understanding and skill**
Know-who – information about who knows what and who knows how to do what	Not explicitly stated under Dearing, but this could be regarded as a key skill. 'Peer assessment' and 'team work' could be used to develop this. Developing these skills encourages students to network and see the strengths of individuals	
These skills would aid the development of all of the above	**Key skills:** communication, numeracy, the use of information technology and learning how to learn	**Personal independence and responsibility**

Apart from the 'know who', which relies on work experience, we can see there is a fairly even mapping across levels of knowledge. This is not really surprising, but does serve to indicate the type of knowledge and skills expected and gives us an understanding of the agendas operating. We can also see that lifelong and independent learning run through all the categories, especially when combined with good reflective skills.

The professionalization of teaching in higher education

Another development worth mentioning is the professionalization of teaching within UK higher education through the Institute for Learning and Teaching. The Institute is a professional membership organization open to all those involved in teaching and teaching support in higher education. The main aim of the Institute is to enhance the status of teaching in higher education, improve the quality of teaching, and set standards of good professional practice. Membership applies to those who can show an understanding of their teaching practice and be reflective in their approach.

Institute for Learning and Teaching

http://www.ilt.ac.uk

The core functions of the ILT are to enhance the status of teaching, improve the experience of learning, and support innovation in higher education. It has also initiated 24 subject centres in the UK that will provide a national learning and teaching support network (LTSN), offering resources and advice on the teaching of these subjects. See section 1.3.3.

Higher Education Funding Council for England (HEFCE)

http://www.hefce.ac.uk

This is a general one-stop site for many aspects of higher education in England. Check here for information on TLTP and FDTL funded projects. See also section 1.3.1.

Scottish Higher Education Funding Council (SHEFC) C&IT Programme

http://www.scotcit.ac.uk

This gives background information to the SHEFC programme with a brief description of projects together with links to reports and planned presentations.

1.2   The learning and teaching agenda

In addition to complying with the economic agenda of providing the right kind of workforce for the next century, we are also seeing changes in educational theory that are becoming equally interested in the learning *process* as well as the content. The process is of course skills-oriented and, if successful, provides lifelong learners with appropriate interpersonal, self-reflective, subject-specific and research skills. Some of the key learning concepts we are dealing with are independent learning, experiential learning, collaborative and cooperative learning, and these are all embedded within a philosophy of education known as *transformative learning*.

There is also more acknowledgement that we all have different styles of learning, and individuals can vary these styles according to how they feel and the subject matter they are learning.

ACTIVITY 1A

What kind of learner are you? Can you recognize these differences in your students?

Consider a topic you want to learn, or one you have recently studied. Look at the learning strategies and cognitive learning styles below. Which would most likely apply to you? Does it vary with the subject you are learning or your experience of the subject?

Learning strategies

1. I will persist until I have thoroughly understood the underlying structure of a topic. I really want to understand what it is all about.

2. I prefer to collect facts, details and examples and then memorize them. I sometimes have difficulty putting down my own thoughts on the subject.

3. I will adapt my learning to the demands of the course and the assignments set.

Cognitive styles of learning

4. I tend to see subjects as a whole, not as separate unrelated items.

5. I take in information in smaller pieces, which I then build up to a whole.

Feedback on the strategies you use as a learner:

Statement 1 – you are a *deep* learner and your aim is to *understand* fully what you are learning.

Statement 2 – you are a *surface* learner and you are concerned with *recalling* facts, as that is the only kind of information you need.

Statement 3 – you are a *strategic* learner who will produce the work that is expected for that learning event, but not beyond.

Feedback on your cognitive style of learning

Statement 4 – you have a cognitive style known as *holistic*. You may have difficulty understanding things as they build up slowly in teaching sessions. As a learner you need the big picture and often you feel your learning appears halted until you have enough information to make sense of it. It is important that teachers don't make such learners feel slow or stupid. You are happy when you have summaries, subheadings, glossary terms, concept maps (anything that will give you the overall structure) to read before getting down to detail.

Statement 5 – you have a cognitive style known as *linear* and find it easier to learn material presented step by step; you are happy understanding small parts before you see the whole picture. You like highly structured courses that take you through the material in small chunks. As you learn each chunk, you gradually build up the whole picture.

Now consider how you teach. Do you tend to limit your teaching according to *your* learning preferences? Do you use the same teaching methods across all topics and for all students?

Consider the kind of teaching you need to accommodate some of these differences. Are you able to accommodate both holistic and linear thinkers?

Please note there are other learning strategies and cognitive styles. This exercise is used to focus on some of these differences and how our own styles of learning may limit our teaching style.

Basics of Effective Learning

Meg Keeley, Bucks County Community College

http://www.bucks.edu/~specpop/index.htm

An excellent site to understand about different kinds of learning. There is a questionnaire to fill in (*Your learning style profile*) with some tips to help you strengthen your particular style. Why not get your students to look at this and determine their learning style? You may then want to use this as the basis of group work – put those with similar cognitive styles and learning strategies together. They may work together much more productively.

1.2.1 Transformative learning

Jack Mezirow first defined his views of transformative learning in 1978, stimulating much discussion between educationalists ever since. Transformative learning is essentially a foundation for a philosophy of adult education. Mezirow's theory is based on a) instrumental learning, and b) communicative learning. Instrumental learning is task-oriented, problem solving, determining cause and effect, learning 'to do' based on empirical analytical discovery. Communicative learning, the essence of transformative learning, is the understanding of meaning of others' values, ideas, feelings and moral decisions and critically examining the assumptions on which these are based, and making decisions. Some of the aspects of transformative learning are illustrated in Figure 1.2.

It is therefore an approach that is concerned with student-centred learning, collaborative learning, the promotion of independent learning/autonomy and exploratory learning through problem solving, and critical reflection within a democratic environment. For a critical review of the literature on transformative learning, see Taylor (1998), who provides a good background for developing an institutional or departmental learning and teaching philosophy around which programmes can be developed.

Independent learning

Independent learning is an overarching concept for the current reforms in higher education. It is not about leaving students to get on with it by themselves, but it is about developing a climate where students are given the space, support and encouragement to become reflective, confident learners. Table 1.2 lists some of the ways we can achieve this.

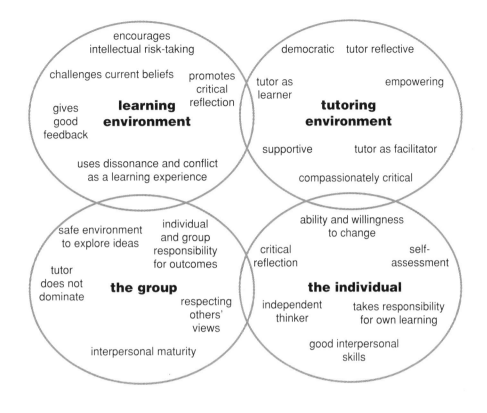

Figure 1.2 *Aspects of transformative learning*

It is important for a department to decide what it means by independent learning if it is going to market this as one of its educational strengths for students.

ACTIVITY 1B

How do we operationalize independent learning?

Some of the questions you may need to ask are:

1. What is independent learning for students in your subject?
   – What skills will such graduates have?
2. How can you operationalize this?
   – How can you change the curriculum design and teaching to implement this?
3. Where are your students now in relation to this view?
4. What transitional changes do you need to put in place?

Table 1.2 *Independent learning*

Student *Some of the factors associated with independent learning:*	Tutor *Some ways of creating a climate to achieve independent learning:*
Be reflective	Build a reflective piece of work into an assessment – this is good for teamwork assignments
Be good at time management	Tutors need an overall view of the amount of work being set so as not to overload students at particular times. Time management skills could be built into study skills' sessions/packs
Take responsibility for your own learning	This is a vital skill – without personal responsibility, independent learning cannot take place. There is a difficult dilemma between 'spoon-feeding' and allowing them to take responsibility. Letting students take responsibility means standing back while they choose to do something you don't like. As a safety measure, always ensure support structures are there and students know about them. Make this aspect very clear from the outset
Monitor own progress	This is part of being a reflective learner. The tutor, however, can set up learning activities that facilitate this. Check out resource-based learning, computer-aided learning and experiential learning in Chapter 3
Know where to get help	Set up a climate of collaboration between students right from the start. Students will know who can help them. You may want to consider how you can reward a good and willing student who seems to be an ideal mentor to other students. In addition, set up clinics and office hours where students can get help from you when necessary
Be a critical thinker	Again, supply students with a variety of perspectives on a topic, encourage a research approach to learning when appropriate and use problem-based and case-based learning to expand and apply their knowledge (see Chapter 3)
Be a team player	It is essential to stress that independent learning is not something that happens in isolation – it is very much the opposite. Encourage collaborative work and a collaborative spirit as independent learning only succeeds when it is truly interdependent. (See Chapters 4 and 5)

5. How will this impact on already validated courses?

6. What impact will this have on teaching staff?

7. Do you need staff development sessions before you can move forward?

Experiential learning

Experiential learning encourages learners to apply the knowledge they have acquired and add to it through direct experience, through role plays, problem solving, case studies, evidence-based learning or work experience. David Kolb's experiential learning cycle is the work that is most often cited in this context and is shown in Figure 1.3. If you are setting up experiential learning, consider this learning cycle and how the elements of the programme can accommodate it.

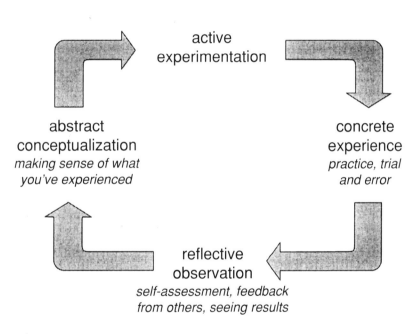

Figure 1.3 *Experiential learning cycle, developed from Kolb*

This approach is firmly embedded in transformative learning, and is also a major component of constructivist learning. Constructivist learning theorists believe that information is not converted to knowledge until individuals 'own' that information and are able to 'construct' it in their own way. Once information and experience are manipulated and changed by individuals (as in Kolb's cycle), they own that knowledge and deep learning is said to have taken place (see section 3.2.1).

Collaborative and cooperative learning

This is an essential element of *communicative learning* within the transformational philosophy. In the literature you will find a difference between these two approaches, which are essentially to do with how much control the lecturer retains in the group and how much 'teaching' goes on. In cooperative learning there is more 'teacher' control; in collaborative learning there is very little. These methods are used differently depending on the purpose of the group and the type of skills to be developed (Matthews *et al*, Web site). This particular teaching and learning method is again high on the agenda for developing interpersonal skills, teamwork and independent learning. Communications technology has been particularly suitable for this type of learning, especially where only asynchronous communication is feasible (see section 4.1.3).

ACTIVITY 1C

Group work

Consider the following statements – how many of them apply to your situation?

1. The average project group size is six.
2. I create a climate where individuals are accountable for the group's outcomes as well as their own contribution.
3. Attention and class time are given to interpersonal/cooperative skill building in the early years of study.
4. When groups have interpersonal problems I encourage them to find their own solutions.
5. We have interactive presentation and feedback sessions for group projects.
6. Students are happy with peer feedback/assessment of their projects.
7. Students keep reflective logs of the group processes in arriving at the outcomes.

Feedback

Statement 1 – a group that is too big can become unwieldy and a group that is too small will not benefit from the challenges of teamwork. Successful groups function at several levels, and according to Bales (1950) these are basically task-oriented and socio-emotional functions. This can impinge on the roles people play within a group, some being more task-oriented and others more integrative (ie, keeping the group happy and functioning). When the group is process- and product-oriented, both these functions become important. A good synopsis of more group functions and stages can be found in Sudweeks and Allbritton (1996) – they then apply this knowledge to computer mediated communication (see section 4.1.3).

Statement 2 – make sure students are clear on what they have to achieve and that they are given the responsibility to do it.

Statement 3 – see the feedback on statement 1. Again this depends on your students. Do they need input for teamworking skills? Do they have some understanding of how teams work in order to get the best out of the experience of the assignment? (See section 5.2 and the reference to the Jolly and Radcliffe Web site.)

Statement 4 – it is easy to come up with solutions for groups when they start to go wrong. You may want to check how much of this to leave to students to sort out for themselves. It is good to facilitate a solution, but if you have given students responsibility, they need to find solutions to interpersonal problems themselves.

Statement 5 – it is always a boost for students if their work is appreciated enough to be given time in class to present it to others. Again it is a follow-through for being responsible for their project. It becomes visible to the rest of the group and therefore valued. They will also be engaging in another key skill – oral presentations. You may want to consider how well equipped they are for doing this – are they aware of the standards expected? (See section 5.3.2.)

Statement 6 – students need to be in agreement with peer assessment systems. Do they decide on the criteria of assessment themselves? Do you suggest some criteria that they accept and/or adapt? Do you tell them the criteria they will use? Whichever system you select, you need to discuss the rationale for it with students (see sections 4.1.6 and 5.3.2).

Statement 7 – an essential part of the transformative learning philosophy is critical self-reflection and a good way of doing this is via reflective logs. It is also important to include this if you are considering assessing the *process* element of group work (see section 5.2 and the reference to Jolly and Radcliffe Web site).

Collaborative Learning

http://www.lgu.ac.uk/deliberations/collab.learning/index.cgi

Centre for Learning and Teaching: Key Skills

Pat Maier, Veronica Oldfield, University of Southampton

http://www.clt.soton.ac.uk

This site offers a wide range of information and links to a wide variety of sources concerned with key skills in the curriculum.

1.3   Supporting these agendas

The following is just a sample of support we are seeing for the current reforms in higher education. The sample taken here is mainly from the UK, but many countries have similar activities. Resources within higher education today are global, and as practitioners we are able to benefit from a great deal of free information dissemination in this field. So, it is unimportant where you are picking your information from, as long as it is of quality and relevant to you.

1.3.1   UK Higher Education Funding Councils

In the UK this agenda for the knowledge economy is being delivered through many funding initiatives of the higher education funding councils (for England: HEFCE, for Scotland: SHEFC, and for Wales: HEFCW). The councils have taken an active role in funding learning and teaching projects with an emphasis on innovation, implementation and dissemination. An important initiative has been the *Teaching & Learning Technology Programme* (TLTP) that is now in its third phase, with funding of approximately £45 million between 1992 and 2001. These projects have ranged from consortia producing individual computer aided learning packages, through the implementation of institutional frameworks for embedding C&IT, to the current third phase where C&IT embedding is occurring both at institutional and national levels. Another initiative, the *Fund for Development of Teaching and Learning* (FDTL), is directly linked to the results departments had from the teaching quality assessment process, and bids for funds can only be made by those departments that demonstrated high quality teaching and learning provision. FDTL is already into phase two with a funding of £12.6 million.

An HEFCE coordinating initiative to begin 2001–2002 is the *Teaching Quality Enhancement Fund* (with a funding of approximately £30 million) which aims to:

> enhance learning and teaching practice, reward high quality, and encourage improvement through funding directed at three different levels – the institution, the subject/discipline, and the individual academic (HEFCE, 1998).

At the institutional level, HEFCE invites bids from those institutions that have demonstrated good provision and success at widening participation to support the implementation of the learning and teaching strategies developed within their institutions. At the subject/discipline level they will combine the FDTL and TLTP projects with this fund to disseminate good practice. In addition, the higher education funding bodies have set up 24 subject centres to share and embed good practice, manage a network of users, and review and promote new materials. This should be a one-stop shop for subject-level use of C&IT innovation. At the individual level, HEFCE will invite higher education institutions to nominate an individual who has excelled in teaching, with those successful receiving grants for teaching research.

This initiative is bringing together the different strands into a coherent strategy that works at the institutional level, tying funding into an institution's learning and teaching strategies: strategies that should be fostering quality and innovation in teaching. We are also seeing that learning technologies are now 'coming of age' and becoming mainstream within the generic issues of learning and teaching, rather than a totally separate strand.

1.3.2 Staff development in the use of C&IT

Several projects under the HEFCE Teaching & Learning Technology Programme Phase Three (TLTP3) are concerned with increasing the uptake of C&IT among staff in higher education. Some of these projects are:

- Teaching and Learning with Network Technologies (TALENT).
- Framework for Optimizing C&IT Uptake and Support (FOCUS).
- Effective Framework for Embedding C&IT using Targeted Support (EFFECTS).

Both TALENT and FOCUS projects are dedicated to the use of learning via the World Wide Web. The TALENT project offers an institution the organizational, educational and technical support and strategies to implement effective Web use for teaching and learning. They have also produced a Web site called 'The Book of Talents' concerned with implementing institutional changes for the use of C&IT. The FOCUS project is also looking at the use of the World Wide Web and is in the process of producing a database that cross-links learning and teaching techniques, software reviews and case studies.

The EFFECTS project particularly addresses the NCIHE (Dearing) Report recommendation 9:

> We recommend that all institutions should, over the medium term, review the changing role of staff as a result of Communications and Information Technology, and ensure that staff and students receive appropriate training and support to enable them to realise its full potential.

This project is developing a series of institutional frameworks that will allow participants to develop their expertise in the educational application of C&IT. They have developed a set of seven generic learning outcomes which will be incorporated into institutional programmes, using a variety of frameworks to do this. Recognition and accreditation for achieving these learning outcomes will come through the institutional programmes that will be recognized by the Institute for Learning and Teaching (ILT). Institutional programmes will, however, need to apply to the ILT for validation, thus closing the 'professional status loop' for teaching in higher education. The consortium is developing various frameworks to achieve these learning outcomes, ranging from traditionally taught courses to autonomous learning via action research projects. The different frameworks have a set of seven learning outcomes in common (see the appendix at the end of Chapter 3). All participants are expected to produce evidence that they have achieved the set learning outcomes through a portfolio of activities. Several of the learning outcomes from this project have been used in the chapters in this book as reflective exercises.

Teaching and Learning with Network Technologies (TALENT)

http://www.le.ac.uk/TALENT/about.htm

Framework for Optimizing C&IT Uptake and Support (FOCUS)

http://www.focus.ac.uk

Effective Framework for Embedding C&IT using Targeted Support (EFFECTS)

http://sh.plym.ac.uk/eds/effects

EFFECTS (Effective Frameworks for Embedding C&IT with Targeted Support) is a national development project working to embed the use of communication and information technologies into the higher education curriculum through programmes of professional development for academic and related staff. EFFECTS will also establish a national accreditation framework so that participants can gain recognition for their achievements and institutions can develop accredited programmes of their own

Netskills Quality Internet Training

http://www.netskills.ac.uk/

Netskills – an ongoing initiative funded by the Joint Information Systems Committee (JISC) – also offers a wide range of workshops for those wishing to use the Web for learning and teaching. Netskills is hosted by the University of Newcastle. It has online materials, resources, and tutorials. The university also offers face-to-face workshops on a regular basis. It has an excellent set of training materials for using the Internet.

1.3.3 Subject support

Subject discipline support comes from a wide range of sources. This section lists a few, predominantly UK in origin. There are more references throughout this book to other relevant sites that are excellent resources for educators.

Support from UK education funding bodies

HEFCE has set up 24 subject centres that address all aspects of learning and teaching across these disciplines. These centres form the Learning and Teaching Support Network (LTSN) designed to be a one-stop shop for all aspects of teaching and learning in that subject. These centres will be the major UK national support for learning and teaching in the subjects.

Learning and Teaching Support Network UK (LTSN)

http://www.ltsn.ac.uk

This is the home site for all the LTS network, providing a link to all subject centres.

Enhancing Learning and Teaching: National Coordination Team

http://www.ncteam.ac.uk/

The National Coordination Team (NCT) works on behalf of the Higher Education Funding Council for England (HEFCE) and the Department for Education Northern Ireland (DENI) to manage and coordinate two initiatives focused on encouraging innovation and new developments within learning and teaching. The initiative – Fund for the Development of Teaching and Learning (FDTL) – is subject-specific. The work of the NCT team focuses on supporting and managing individual projects, creating project networking opportunities, maintaining effective communication between the initiatives, and promoting the work of the two initiatives within higher education.

Directory of Networked Resources

http://www.niss.ac.uk/subject/

In addition to projects there is also a source of help funded under the JISC (Joint Information Systems Committee) in connection with the electronic libraries projects (eLib projects). These are *information gateways* that house – as a library – validated resources for particular subjects. Some of the gateways are: SOSIG for social sciences, EEVL for engineering, OMNI for medicine. For a full list, refer to this Web site.

Support from UK research funding bodies

The example taken for this section is the Economic & Social Research Council (ESRC). It currently has a £2 million budget to examine the nature of the emerging *learning society*. In line with this there is also the *Virtual Society?* strand. Traditionally the education funding bodies tend to fund projects that address the practitioner, whereas ESRC tends to have more pure research projects. However, it also has a strand of research entitled *Teaching and Learning Research Programme* (£12.5 million) with interdisciplinary teams including practitioners and learners.

Economic & Social Research Council (ESRC)

http://www.esrc.ac.uk

Select the 'thematic priorities' to see the strands of research being funded. Of interest to readers might be the 'Knowledge, Communications & Learning' theme. Within this theme are a series of 'Learning Society' projects, covering areas such as 'lifelong learning' and 'knowledge society'. You can follow links to information on the projects that are funded in this field.

Virtual Society? (ESRC)

http://www.brunel.ac.uk/research/virtsoc

This site has all information regarding Virtual Society? projects. It also has other links to all things 'virtual'.

Support from European Union funding bodies

There are a wide variety of EU projects in this area, Leonardo da Vinci and Socrates being just two initiatives. There is no space to delve into these projects here, but the reader can find out more from CORDIS.

CORDIS

http://www.cordis.lu/

This is the Community Research and Development Information Service. Check out this site for a variety of programmes.

Other sources of support

Online journals, magazines, resources from projects and universities' own pages are becoming excellent resources for the whole education community. Here are some examples.

UltiBASE

http://ultibase.eu.rmit.edu.au/index.html

This Australian site is hosted by RMIT University and comprises a peer reviewed journal, teaching and learning materials, as well as national and international events. It acts as a publishing medium for those interested in writing articles on the learning and teaching agenda.

Higher-Ed.Org

http://www.higher-ed.org/

This is an American site hosting a wide range of resources in higher education. They link to publications in higher education, universities' strategic plans, online journals, jobs in higher education, research centres, etc.

 ERIC Clearinghouse on Higher Education

http://www.eriche.org/About/index.html

The Educational Resources Information Center (ERIC) is a national information system designed to provide users with ready access to an extensive body of education-related literature. ERIC, established in 1966, is supported by the US Department of Education, Office of Educational Research and Improvement, and the National Library of Education.

 DeLiberations

http://www.lgu.ac.uk/deliberations

DeLiberations is an interactive online magazine designed to act as a resource for educational developers, librarians, academic staff and managers in education, with material arranged by discipline and by educational issue. It is also a forum for readers to discuss and develop ideas, and identify resources that will aid their work. DeLiberations runs a parallel mailing list at mailbase, deliberations-forum as a further arena for discussion.

 COPAC

http://copac.ac.uk/copac/about.html

This site gives you access to online catalogues of some of the largest university research libraries in the UK and Ireland.

 Active Learning

http://www.cti.ac.uk/publ/actlea/

This is a refereed journal offering articles on C&IT written by practitioners in the field of higher education. Back copies of articles are freely available on the site.

 New Academic: the magazine of teaching and learning in higher education

http://www.seda.demon.co.uk/newacad.html

This magazine is paper-based and obtained from SEDA (Staff & Educational Development Association). It contains generic educational articles rather than those dedicated to C&IT, as with *Active Learning*.

 First Monday

http://www.firstmonday.dk/

This is a peer reviewed online journal on generic aspects of education.

📖 **World Lecture Hall**

http://www.utexas.edu/world/lecture

This site from the University of Texas contains links to pages created by faculties worldwide which are using the Web to deliver class materials. This is supported by members and there is a form if you want to add something.

📖 **Mailbases**

http://www.mailbase.ac.uk

Mailbase is a wide selection of national and international academic discussion groups. Simply go to the site and search for a topic of interest. Follow the links and it will tell you how to join the group. If you don't wish to join, you can still read the contributions via the Web site. However, this is not the spirit of it – the success of the groups is the active members.

References

Bales, R F (1950) *An Interactive Process Analysis: A method for the study of small groups*, Addison-Wesley, Reading, MA

HEFCE (1998) 'HEFCE plans to promote high quality and widen participation in higher education', Press Release 18 August, http://www.hefce.ac.uk/News/HEFCE/default.htm

HEFCE (1999) *Performance Indicators in Higher Education in the UK*, Report 99/66, http://www.niss.ac.uk/education/hefce/pub99/99_66/main.html#intro

Kolb, D (1984) *Experience as the Source of Learning and Development*, Prentice-Hall, Maidenhead

Lubbers, R F M (1999a) *The Globalization of Economy and Society*, http://www.globalize.org/publications/globview.html

Lubbers, R F M (1999b) *The Dynamic of Globalization*, http://www.globalize.org/publications/dynamic.html

Matthews, R S, Cooper, J L, Davidson, N and Hawkes, P, *Building Bridges Between Cooperative and Collaborative Learning*, http://www2.emc.maricopa.edu/innovation/CCL/building.html

National Committee of Inquiry into Higher Education (1997) *Higher Education in the Learning Society*, chaired by Sir Ron Dearing, http://www.leeds.ac.uk/educol/ncihe/

OECD (1996) *The Knowledge-based Economy*, http://www.oecd.org/dsti/sti/s_t/inte/prod/kbe.htm

OECD (1997) *Graduate Output of Educational Institutions*, http://www.oecd.org/els/stats/eag97/chapterg.htm

Panitz, T (1996) *A Definition of Collaborative vs Cooperative Learning*, published by DeLiberations, http://www.lgu.ac.uk/deliberations/collab.learning/panitz2.html

Sudweeks, F and Allbritton, M (1996) 'Working together apart: communication and collaboration in a networked group', in eds C D Keen, C Urquhart and J Lamp, *Proceedings of the 7th Australasian Conference of Information Systems* (ACIS96), Vol. 2, Department of Computer Science, University of Tasmania, pp.701–12, http://www.arch.usyd.edu.au/~fay/papers/acis96.html

Taylor, E (1998) *Theory and Practice of Transformative Learning*, ERIC Clearinghouse on Adult, Career and Vocational Education, Ohio State University, http://ericacve.org/mp_taylor_01.asp

Thorne, M (1999) 'Fierce competition in the virtual, global game', *The Times Higher Education Supplement*, 5 November

2 Developing new teaching skills

As a result of the new agendas and the reforms taking place globally in higher education, we are now having to reassess how we feel about this and how we should change our teaching. This chapter:

- looks closely at how our teaching is changing, how we feel about it and how we can adapt (2.1);
- offers a checklist to help you assess whether you, your students and your institution are ready to make use of C&IT (2.2);
- presents the types of multimedia resource available and their uses, advantages and disadvantages (2.3).

2.1 The changing model of learning and teaching

The 'traditional' view of higher education sees highly intelligent and well motivated students debating in intimate seminar groups, studying in quiet, well-stocked libraries and experimenting in advanced laboratories. As we all know, this 'Oxbridge ideal' is a figment of our culture's imagination and bears little relation to most students' experiences. Today's reality is one in which mass higher education, flexible modes of study and widening participation are becoming the rule rather than the exception.

As a result we are seeing a shift in learning and teaching models across the education sector that lessens the tutor–student bond and increases student independence and interdependence between one another. However, this shift is not solely concerned with increasing student numbers, but also with an awareness that students need to be equipped with the intellectual and interpersonal skills necessary for a knowledge-based economy which relies on the adaptability and hence the learning skills of its workforce. It is very much a learning society that is increasingly dependent on electronic information and communications, where large quantities of material are available on demand and transactions can take place remotely. It is at this intersection that education and commerce converge.

Methods of teaching and learning are now reflecting these changes, providing a more holistic approach involving the development of:

- content (the knowledge base);
- intellectual skills (critical thinking, problem solving, creativity);
- learning skills (developing the independent learner, reflective practice);
- personal and interpersonal skills (time management, communication).

Today we can no longer exclusively emphasize the course content to be learnt. We need to make all the skills we teach, which have very often been implicit up until now, explicit. This means that what we expect students to learn on our course should be stated as learning outcomes. Some of those learning outcomes may be achieved through traditional didactic methods, while others may be achieved by setting up group projects, poster exhibitions, role plays and simulations. In essence, the content alone, as a series of facts, is no longer sufficient. Cross (1995) claims that half the content on a five-year medical programme may be obsolete by the time students graduate.

Making that link between observing our own practice and understanding the changes in society can be difficult and daunting. How do we feel about this? Do we feel that education should not be influenced by these 'trends', or are we enthused by it? Where do we start?

ACTIVITY 2A

Identifying your skills

1. What makes *you* an independent learner?

Your characteristics for independent learning

Check the balance here between subject knowledge and skills for learning. How did *you* learn these skills? How could you help your students develop a similar generic set of skills more efficiently? How could your teaching change to accommodate this?

Your characteristics for employment success

2. As an academic/teacher/tutor, list the skills you need to be successful in your job.

Check the balance needed between the knowledge of your subject and skills. Are there any aspects you feel you would like to develop? How could you help your students develop a similar generic set of skills more efficiently? How could your teaching change to accommodate this?

ACTIVITY 2B

How do you feel about your students being more independent?

	Agree	Not sure	Disagree
I will lose control of my students' learning.	❏	❏	❏
Independence in learning encourages independent thought.	❏	❏	❏
The quality of the course will suffer.	❏	❏	❏

	Agree	Not sure	Disagree
It is just one way of telling students to 'go away and get on with it'.	❑	❑	❑
It will take up a lot of time to set up correctly.	❑	❑	❑
It will give students the necessary employability skills they need.	❑	❑	❑
I would enjoy developing this kind of teaching.	❑	❑	❑
Many students would suffer if I left them on their own.	❑	❑	❑
Independent learning can satisfy the learning styles of a wider range of students.	❑	❑	❑

Feedback

Do you see yourself as central to your students' learning and happy with the teaching strategies that allow you to keep control?

Do you see yourself as not central to your students' learning and happy with teaching strategies that give independence to your students?

Do you see yourself as someone who needs to control some aspects of your students' learning while allowing them independence at other times?

Any of these opinions may be correct for a given situation. However, whatever your current teaching methods, stop and think about how your students develop 'all round' skills from your courses. If you would like to introduce more independent learning but find your students hostile, you will need to consider a step-by-step approach that slowly increases their independence. Be sure to give plenty of support during this phase.

We tend to aim for more control when numbers are large in an attempt to create structure and focus for the group. In order to do this, we have to encourage independent learning, for example by using resource-based learning approaches. This will mean more work initially to set up the resources, but it should pay off in later years as students develop their independence. In this model of learning and teaching (see Figure 2.1) we are moving away from being dispensers of information to being facilitators of change who encourage students' lifelong learning skills – a process of continual 'transformation'.

A Fresh Look at Independent Learning

Phil Race (1996)

http://www.lgu.ac.uk/deliberations/eff.learning/indep.html

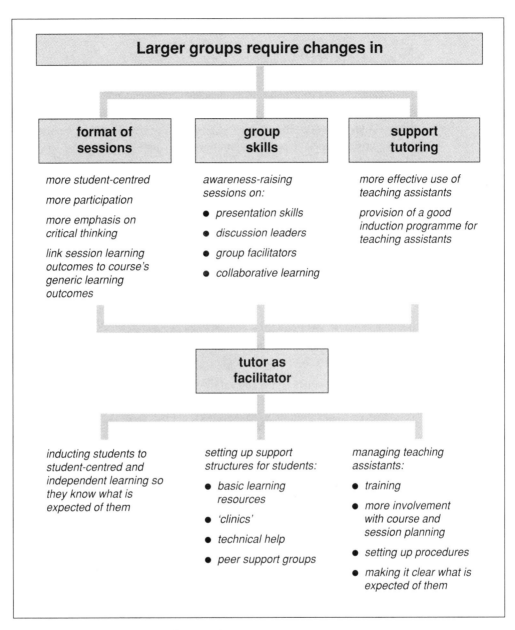

Figure 2.1 *Managing teaching in large groups*

ACTIVITY 2C

What changes could you make?

Use the reflective activities (2A and 2B) above to consider how you teach and any changes you may want to introduce to make your teaching more 'holistic', covering both content and lifelong learning skills (independent learning, personal development). Some aspects you may consider are:

- Tutor becomes facilitator or guide to the learning process.
- Students are expected to become more independent (seriously consider what this means for you and your department and how it can be realized without students feeling they are being neglected).
- Students work more collaboratively with peers and less competitively – group and team-work (this will impinge on your modes of assessment).
- Students become more reflective of their learning process (build in assessment of both process and product of students' work).

A wide variety of terminology has been used to cover the area of independent learning, with a great deal of conceptual overlap. You have probably heard most of these terms before, but Figure 2.2 gives a handy summary.

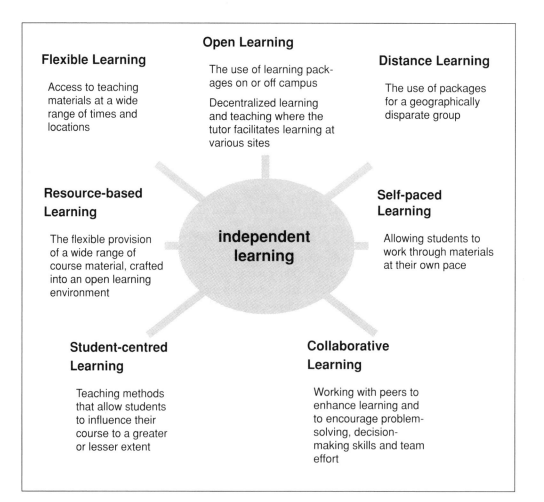

Figure 2.2   *Common ways to support independent learning*

Open and distance education are no longer restricted to UK institutions like the Open University, the Open College or company training schemes. We are increasingly seeing traditional universities offer flexible distance and part-time courses. The concept of the 'virtual university', where distance learning concepts are fully embedded within learning technologies, is much broader than the traditional distance learning programme, primarily located within one university. In the future, as global education increases, we may see networks of traditional universities forming a virtual university where students can gain credits towards an accredited programme that is validated by the university network. In addition, global education will not be restricted to universities and already we are seeing companies like PricewaterhouseCoopers advertising its own 'virtual university' on the World Wide Web. Hybrid organizations like the University for Industry (UfI), a public/private partnership set up by the Department for Education and Employment in the UK, will promote flexible training material from companies and universities to service the industrial sector.

The Virtual University Association

http://www.virtualuniversity.com/default.html

Explains the purpose of virtual universities and how to create one.

Mailbase: Virtual-Universities

http://www.mailbase.ac.uk

Select 'discussion lists' and then 'V' from the menu and search until you find the 'Virtual-Universities' group. This group discusses issues such as online standards, teacher education, evaluating Internet resources, online collaboration, and creating online materials.

UfI – University for Industry – LearnDirect

http://www.ufiltd.co.uk/ and http://www.learningdirect.org

LearnDirect is the name of the UfI's network of learning centres that are being set up in the UK. Eventually over 1000 centres will provide computer-based flexible learning resources in easily accessible locations such as shopping centres, sports centres and clubs, community centres, churches and railways stations. Some will also be based with large employers.

Open University Homepage (UK)

http://www.open.ac.uk/

Extramural Open University Study (New Zealand)

http://www.massey.ac.nz/

Select extramural enrolment.

United States Open University

http://www.open.edu/

Open Learning Australia

http://www.ola.edu.au/

 International Centre for Distance Learning (ICDL)

http://obelix.open.ac.uk/

Contains information on over 31,000 distance learning programmes worldwide.

Computer technology is becoming increasingly essential to this new learning and teaching model, where more students have access to higher education and where delivery can be flexible and encourage independent learning. This increases the need for those vital lifelong learning skills.

The remainder of the book will discuss how we can start using C&IT in our own teaching and develop some of the strategies mentioned above.

2.2 Essential requirements for all users of C&IT

Before you start planning to use computer-based resources or electronic communications to support learning and teaching, there are some essential requirements that must be met by you and your students if your plans are to be successful:

- staff and student access to suitable computers;
- basic computing skills; and
- adequate technical support.

2.2.1 Staff access to suitable computers

Do you and your teaching assistants have regular and convenient access to suitable computers? Do you have a personal computer in your office? Suitability includes:

- *The computer system's specification*: does it have to be a modern PC running Windows 95/98 or are Apple Macs and older PCs running Windows 3.1 acceptable? Are a CD ROM and printer required?
- *An Internet connection* via a local area network (LAN) if you want to use *e-mail* or the *Web*. If you do not have a connection you will need to talk to your departmental IT support officer or your institution's computing service, since connecting a PC to a network and configuring it so it works are tasks for experts.
- If you are planning to use multimedia, your PC may need to have additional hardware and software. If you want to use:
  - *digital images* you will need an image scanner or digital camera;
  - *digital audio* you will need a sound card and speakers or headphones, plus a microphone and/or cassette tape player;

– *digital video* you will need an advanced graphics card in your PC and a video recorder or camcorder.

Some institutions have media studios with all this equipment freely available for use by staff, so find out about this before buying your own.

● *The software installed:* the basics are a modern word-processor and presentation program, a Web browser and e-mail. An up-to-date anti-virus program is also essential. After that, it depends what you want to do – spreadsheets, databases, graphics, image processing, Web-site publishing, statistics and so on.

Here are some other things you need to think about:

● Note that your institution may only support specific programs, and it is probably always a good idea to follow their recommendations so you can get help if you need it. Always ask your computing service if there are any special deals available, such as a 'site licence' that allows you to install the software for free. A lot of software also has excellent educational prices available through the CHEST licensing arrangement within the UK.

● If you share a computer with other staff, problems will arise if you start to make regular extensive use of it to develop digital resources or manage electronic communications. You may be able to make a case for your department to buy you your own PC, or you may be forced to buy your own!

● If you are creating resources to be used in your teaching, check the availability of the equipment in the room to be used. You may be able to borrow or have the equipment brought to you wherever you need it – for example your institution's audio-visual support unit may have a small stock of data projectors that can be booked in advance. If the equipment is already in the room, make sure you know how it works *before* the first session – and watch out for unexpected room changes next term!

2.2.2   Student access to institutional computers

Will the students need to use computers at your institution, or are they required to have suitable computers themselves? If you intend your students to use computers at your institution, you need to check that they meet your needs:

● *Are there enough computers?* In an ideal world the computer:student ratio would be 1:1. We know this is not possible, but we should only consider using computers if there are enough of them for the students to use at a convenient place and time, otherwise they will just get frustrated and irritated by the whole process. As a rough guide, one PC for every 10 students is an acceptable ratio. However, the more students are expected to use computers, the lower this ratio should be.

● *Access restrictions.* Perhaps your institution has a good ratio of computers to students, but you may find that most of the time the computer rooms are booked out for classes, or their closing time is 8pm. If booking is the only real solution, then consider doing that for your students. It is less flexible this way, but there is some guaranteed access. Don't rely on ratio figures given to you by your institution: check the *real* availability to students. You may have to do some lobbying to get unfavourable conditions changed.

- *Poor locations.* Some computer rooms may be difficult for your students to get to; for example they may be off campus. Once again it is important to gain a view of the *real* availability to students. Sometimes these 'out of the way' locations are badly furnished, have poor lighting and older PCs – not a very inviting place to study.

- *The specification of the computers.* You may find you want to provide multimedia resources such as audio or video, but only a few (or none) of the computers can run these. Check with your computing services department what you can realistically offer your students – it may be that a simple software upgrade is all that is needed to deliver some types of multimedia.

2.2.3 Student access using home computers

Many students have their own PCs, often bought to avoid the access problems associated with institutional computers. Having their own PC means that they can study and work in their room whenever they want, have all their books handy, talk to their friends, eat and drink, take a break without losing their place and listen to music. However, not all students have the money or the inclination to buy a PC, so you cannot rely on them unless they are a course requirement – and that is still rare in the UK. More courses will take this approach as computer use by students grows and puts ever-increasing pressure on institutional resources. The requirements will have to specify the minimum hardware and software. For example a Pentium PC with a 200 MHz processor, 32 MB memory, CD ROM, Windows 95 and Microsoft Word 97 is an out-of-date system but is definitely adequate for most purposes and would allow the use of cheap second-hand systems.

Specifying access to the Internet from students' rooms is a much trickier problem since it requires a fixed phone line. There may be a single phone line into a student house, but using it for long Internet calls will cause arguments over bills and access. Note that students living in shared accommodation may use a mobile phone instead and the personal fixed phone line necessary for a modem represents a large additional expense.

Students will also need an account with an Internet Service Provider (ISP) such as BT, America Online, Freeserve or CompuServe. There are many 'free' ISPs in the UK that provide Internet access for the cost of a local phone call. Naturally, your students will have to bear the cost of these calls, so you will need to think about the implications of this.

There are groups of students for whom Internet access using home PCs is a realistic option, notably mature part-time and distance learners. These people are much more likely to have their own home with a phone line, and studying using the Internet may be one of the major selling points of the course since it allows them to conveniently study in their spare time, fitting around their work and family commitments.

Another group who may see Internet access as a major benefit are students with disabilities, since it should allow them to take control of their modes of study. For example, dyslexic students can use screen-readers to listen to text-based resources. There are government grants available to help them buy the equipment and pay for the connection charges.

2.2.4 Students with disabilities

You have a legal and moral obligation to ensure that your course is open to anyone, regardless of any physical disabilities they may have. Some of you may already have had to make changes to accommodate a disabled student, hopefully with assistance from your institution's disability support unit.

It is worth thinking about the fact that making your courses more accessible to students with disabilities will benefit *all* the students. For example, dyslexia is one of the most common disabilities that affects learning, yet most courses are predominantly text-based. If you present some resources visually, that will also help others understand, particularly those who favour a visual learning style.

If you start to make use of electronic resources you will need to pay careful attention to accessibility. There are simple guidelines that you can follow that will make your resources available to as wide an audience as possible. For example, you can design your Web pages so they can be easily heard and navigated by visually impaired or dyslexic students using a text-to-speech converter with their Web browser.

This is an important issue we cannot overlook, as most institutions have an accessibility statement for 'inclusivity'. The UK Quality Assurance Agency has developed a *Code of Practice* as a guide for institutions in this area (see reference below). Always check your student intake to find out if there are any who have hearing, visual or physical impairments or dyslexia that prevent them gaining full access to your materials. It is good to check with the disabilities officer in your institution.

Quality Assurance Agency for Higher Education (UK)

Code of Practice for Assurance of Academic Quality & Standards in Higher Education: Students with Disabilities

http://www.qaa.ac.uk/COPswd1/foreword.htm

This code of practice recognizes that disabled students are an integral part of the academic community. It takes as its starting point the premise that accessible and appropriate provision is not 'additional', but a core element of the overall service that an institution makes available. As such, the quality of the learning opportunities on offer to disabled students in higher education institutions needs to be assured in the same way as any other provision.

DISinHE

http://www.disinhe.ac.uk/resources/guides/

This is an excellent site with a series of 'Good Practice Guides' such as *Guidelines for accessible courseware, designing teaching and learning technology, disability and new technology: A guide for lecturers.*

The Adaptive Technology Resource Centre

University of Toronto

http://www.utoronto.ca/atrc/index.html

There is a technical glossary page listing the types of technology available – useful to get an overview. These technologies are referred to as either 'adaptive' or 'assistive' technologies.

Services for Students with Disabilities

http://ats.tamu.edu/Default.htm

Texas A&M University. This is an example of a university taking the issue seriously and this Web site shows how they are doing it.

Bobby

http://www.cast.org/bobby/

Bobby is a Web-based tool that analyses Web pages for their accessibility to people with disabilities. CAST offers Bobby as a free public service in order to further its mission to expand opportunities for people with disabilities through the innovative uses of computer technology. To analyse your Web site, type in the URL of the page that you want Bobby to examine and click Submit. Bobby will display a report indicating any accessibility and/or browser compatibility errors found on the page. Once your site receives a Bobby Approved rating, you are entitled to display a Bobby Approved icon on your site. This service is being used increasingly by educational Web sites.

DO IT

University of Washington

http://www.washington.edu/doit/Resources/web-design.html

There is a wide range of links for accessible Web page design. This address links directly to these resources – simply follow the home icon to return to the homepage.

2.2.5   Do we have sufficient computing skills?

Does everyone (including yourself and your teaching assistants) have the skills needed to operate the computers? These skills include basic computing and file management, adequate typing ability, and a little background knowledge. Ideally, everyone should know how to use a word-processor and e-mail and how to surf the Web.

If you or your students lack these skills, can your institution provide appropriate training in time? If tutor-led training is provided, there may be problems with the timing of the courses or limited availability of places. Alternatively, self-paced, self-study materials may be provided either as workbooks or computer-based learning. You will need to think about the time needed to acquire these skills, not just in hours of study but the weeks that those hours are spread over.

If you are planning to use an online discussion group, you will probably need to give your students a short training session so they know how to access the discussion and send, read and reply to messages. This should preferably be right at the start of the course so that it is relevant and they can start practising their newly learnt skills immediately. The need for this training will disappear as more courses include online groups and students become familiar with their use, especially if institutions standardize the software they use.

2.2.6 Can we get adequate technical support?

Is adequate technical support available to you? If the discussion group software or Web site becomes unreliable or inaccessible, you need to know who to contact so that it can be fixed quickly. This will usually be the institution's computing service or learning technology support unit. If no support is available, you can still use online learning technologies, but the risk of failure is greater.

Your institution's computing service will work hard to ensure that all their public-access computers, servers and network infrastructure remain operational. However, you should always be aware that problems can occur and take a day or so to fix. They may also provide some central computing support for staff and students.

Technical support for students using their own computers at home is much more problematic. They will either have to pay a computer supplier to fix any problems or persuade a knowledgeable friend to help. Distance learners should be encouraged to contact you by phone or letter within a week if they have ongoing computer problems. If your course provides technical support for these distance learners, if only by phone or e-mail, the person responsible should respond to requests as quickly as possible, even if finding the solution takes much longer.

2.2.7 Procedures for putting programs and other resources on to a network

Your institution's computing service will have procedures for putting resources on to the network so that computing staff can maintain the system effectively, ensure that software is properly licensed and control viruses. There may also be procedures that regulate the material that is published on institutional Web sites so that standards can be maintained and copyright and legal issues checked. Check with your institution to find out about these procedures in plenty of time, since you may find that new software can only be installed on the public computers during infrequent scheduled upgrades. Do check this.

Time and know-how for you to do this

- Identify the resources you have in terms of text, images (photos, diagrams, pictures) and media (video, sound).
- Do you have to worry about copyright clearance? (See section 2.4.)
- Do you know how to get these resources on to the computer? Can you get advice or help in finding the software and then learning how to use it? Check that you can run the chosen software on your computer.

● How much time do you think you'll need? Is that feasible? Like so many jobs, digitizing resources always takes twice as long as you hoped!

2.2.8 Three things you *must* do to avoid disaster

There are many reasons why computers can and do go wrong, ranging from broken hardware, through software bugs, to the all-too-common user error. Provided you take the right precautions, these problems will be merely inconvenient. If you don't think ahead, however, any problem can turn into a major disaster. For example, suppose you have been working hard producing resources for a course using your computer. You have spent more hours than you care to think of typing the course outline, learning objectives, lesson plans, assignments and test questions. Then you discover, a week before the course starts, that a virus has infected your computer and corrupted all the files. It is vital to take precautions.

You must have an up-to-date *anti-virus program* installed on your PC. It will constantly keep an eye on your other programs in case they show signs of infection and can disinfect programs and document files. You have to update the software at least twice a year because new viruses are constantly appearing, but the updates can be easily downloaded from the Web. Ask your computing service which program it recommends.

The second thing you have to do is to keep copies of all your important files on disk. If the copy on your computer is deleted or damaged, you can restore the copy from the *backup* disk. Ideally, you should take a copy of the files that you have been working on at the end of each day, but that is probably a counsel of perfection. Realistically you should back up your new or edited files every week. Windows has a backup utility program that can be used to automate this process.

It doesn't take many files to fill a 3.5 inch floppy disk, so you should invest in a high-capacity removable drive, such as a ZIP drive or an LS-120. These have a capacity of around 100 megabytes – enough for plenty of files. The best option is a re-writable CD-RW drive that has a capacity of 650 megabytes. All these devices make a daily backup a simple task using automated backup software. The Active*Guide has further advice about backup techniques.

It may be that your office PC is attached to a departmental server via the local area network. If so, find out if the server has a backup taken every night (most do) and if you can copy your files to a directory on the server. The Windows backup utility can automate the copying of all new and updated files to the server with just a double-click.

The third thing you need to do is have a *routine* for backing up your files – and stick to it! If you only do it every now and again, any disaster is bound to find you with your last backup six weeks out-of-date – which either means six weeks of work lost forever or a lot of retyping from your printed copies.

ACTIVITY 2D

Analyse the opportunities and constraints in using C&IT, and select C&IT appropriate to the learning situation you have chosen

You could:

- carry out an IT audit to identify resource availability;
- identify the constraints within your institution (department);
- analyse the learning needs of students regarding the use of selected C&IT.

(Taken from the EFFECTS programme – see the Appendix to Chapter 3 for the seven generic learning outcomes used on the programme, and Chapter 1 for information about the EFFECTS programme.)

2.3　Creating multimedia resources

The whole area of computers in education can be very daunting, and at this stage it may be wise to clarify where we see computers being used in education – see Figure 2.3.

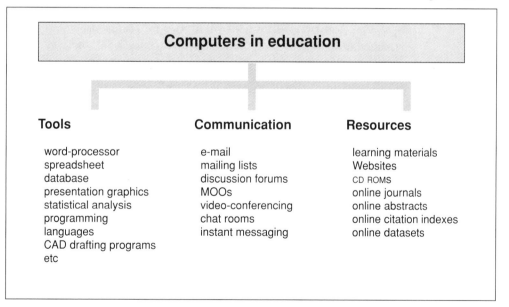

Figure 2.3　*Computers in education*

Most disciplines have their specific IT 'tools of the trade', such as a word-processor, spreadsheet or statistics program. However, when we come to use 'computers in education' we find we generally want to use them for *resources* and/or *communications*. So, when you want to consider using C&IT in education, decide first if it is as a resource, for communication purposes or a mixture of the two. In addition to this, of course, determine the specific IT tools used in your discipline.

Since technology is both a production and a dissemination medium, the resources we create for teaching can easily be made available to students for learning. Because they are digitized and available via a network, they are flexibly and permanently accessible, and can be easily updated as they age. This allows students to revisit the material as often as they need and gives them support. It also encourages them to use C&IT to access course materials and gives them confidence to search further for more resources.

We may already have some good examples of teaching aids in our rooms, such as:

- artefacts (models, samples);
- images (photos, diagrams, x-rays, video);
- simulations (manipulating models, processes);
- 'skeleton' notes from lectures (could be overhead transparencies);
- quizzes, exercises and questions.

We are not advocating that all teaching aids become digital, as seeing and touching the 'real' thing can be very important. However, many of our teaching aids can be digitized and stored on a computer. Once we have them there we are free to use them in more flexible ways.

Before we can use multimedia resources or make them available to students, we have to store them in a digital format so they can be accessed using computers. The next few sections outline how multimedia assets are produced, the level of effort required and their advantages and disadvantages. An indication of the effort required for each resource is shown in Table 2.1.

Table 2.1

Multimedia resource	effort to create
Word-processed documents	■ ❑ ❑ ❑ ❑
Presentations	■ ❑ ❑ ❑ ❑
Digital images	■ ■ ❑ ❑ ❑
Graphics and clip-art	■ ■ ■ ❑ ❑
Web pages	■ ■ ■ ❑ ❑
Digital audio	■ ■ ■ ❑ ❑
Digital video	■ ■ ■ ■ ❑
Simulations	■ ■ ■ ■ ■
Key:	
simple technology, low effort	■ ❑ ❑ ❑ ❑
complex technology, high effort	■ ■ ■ ■ ■

Whenever you make use of multimedia, always make sure that you are clear about the educational purpose it serves. There is nothing more irritating than waiting for a resource to download over the Internet only to wonder at its relevance when it arrives. Remember that it also takes effort to create the resources in the first instance, so choose them carefully and create guidance notes to help students use them intelligently.

2.3.1 Word-processed documents

■ ❑ ❑ ❑ ❑

Advantages

- Gives a professional and clearly legible appearance to course materials.
- Documents can be easily edited and updated, reflecting feedback and your developing ideas about the course.
- Documents can include tables, diagrams, pictures, charts and equations.
- If distributed and viewed using a computer, documents can also include multimedia files such as colour photos, audio and video clips.
- Live links to Web sites, to other documents or to other parts of the same document are also possible. These links are excellent for guiding students to relevant Web resources.
- Modern word-processors enable you to save a document as a Web page, ready to publish on a Web site. It is as simple as choosing *Save As* from the program's *File* menu and selecting the *Web page (HTML)* file type.
- You can print directly from your PC on to OHP transparencies (OHTs). Make sure you follow the rules for good presentation design available on the Active*Guide.
- You can produce documents that use colour, provided you have a low-cost colour inkjet printer. However, the cost and speed of printing mean that you will not usually want to print a copy for every student.

Disadvantages

- It often takes longer to produce the first version of a handout, especially if it involves equations or diagrams – but updating it is always much quicker.

Equipment required

- A computer with standard word-processing software.
- A reasonably good printer, either a laser printer or colour inkjet printer.
- A photocopier – preferably one that can automatically produce double-sided, collated and stapled handouts from your stack of single-sided printouts.
- OHTs – make sure you buy the correct transparencies for your printer, since inkjet and laser printers need different types of transparencies.
- An OHP to project the OHTs.

Comments

Generally speaking, most tutors (and students) are competent word-processor users. However, if you are starting out, check which word-processing software your institution supports and if there are any training materials or courses to help you.

You will still need to photocopy and distribute the handouts to the students, unless you expect to make them available via the Web, in which case students can either read them on screen or print them out. However, since almost everyone prefers to use paper documents, you are effectively transferring the printing costs (and time) from your department to the individual students.

Ideally, your software should be able to produce files that can be read by your students' software. For example, if you use Word 2000, you should save files using the older Word 97 format unless you are certain that they all use the latest version of Word as well. If in doubt, distribute files as RTF (Rich Text Format).

Well-produced handouts indicate a professional approach to the students as learners and set a standard for students' own work. Many tutors insist on word-processed essays to ensure that they can read what has been written and avoid wasting time trying to decipher illegible handwriting.

Students can hand in word-processed documents that include multimedia objects and hyperlinks. The era of the multimedia essay is upon us, although deciding what criteria to use for assessment may be a challenge. What value do the multimedia elements add to the text and how do they illuminate the understanding and knowledge of the author?

2.3.2 Presentations

■ ❑ ❑ ❑ ❑

Computer presentation software such as Microsoft PowerPoint can be used to:

- prepare printed OHTs to support a lecture;
- display the slides using a computer and data projector;
- publish the slides as Web pages;
- produce poster displays;
- create diagrams.

Most professional and conference talks are now prepared and delivered with the help of presentation software. The software is simple to use and allows you to easily add, edit and rearrange slides as you think through what you want to say – in other words, the act of creating the presentation helps you develop your talk.

Advantages

- Presentation software comes with design templates that instantly add a professional look to your slides. You can easily create your own templates to define an institutional, departmental, or personal 'look' that can be applied to any presentation.

- The slides can be edited and reorganized when the presentation needs to be updated. This can be done literally minutes before the talk, if need be.
- The slides can include text, images, diagrams and charts. These are either created using the software or imported from another program (for example, a chart from a spreadsheet program).
- The slides can be presented using an OHP once you have printed them as black and white OHTs using a laser printer, or as colour OHTs using a colour inkjet printer. Remember to use the right sort of transparency film for the type of printer you are using.
- The slides can also be printed out on paper as student handouts, three or six to a side to save paper. Students really appreciate these since they can concentrate on what you say and add their own notes to the handouts.
- You can also create your own speaker notes based on your slides, which include facts, quotes, references and prompts not on the slides themselves.
- The slides can be presented directly from a computer if you have a projection device (see *equipment required*). This means that you can make use of colour, animation effects and multimedia – colour photos, sound and video clips.
- If presenting using a computer, selected slides can easily be 'hidden' or 'unhidden' to customize the presentation to a specific audience. Links can be added that enable jumps to different parts of the presentation, allowing you to change your talk depending on feedback from the audience.
- Presentation software comes with drawing tools that enable you to create neat and attractive diagrams. You can draw rectangles, circles, text and arrows as well as more complex shapes. A huge range of clip-art pictures is available to instantly illustrate almost any topic – for example medical illustrations. These diagrams can include simple animation effects if you present using a computer.
- Presentations can be easily saved as a set of Web pages, ready for publishing on a Web site – see Figure 2.4. Each slide has its own page and you can add more information below the slide if you wish, such as comments, tasks to do or links to other Web pages.
- Presentation software can also be used to prepare posters and signs of all types and sizes.

Disadvantages

- The use of OHTs or computer presentations can result in inflexible talks that cannot easily be adjusted in response to audience feedback.
- The dynamic act of drawing a diagram on a whiteboard or OHT is sometimes more effective than showing a static pre-drawn diagram.

Equipment required

- A relatively modern PC or Apple Mac. It is more convenient if this is your own portable (laptop) computer, even if a PC is already available at your venue. The more types of multimedia you use, the more modern and powerful the computer you will need.

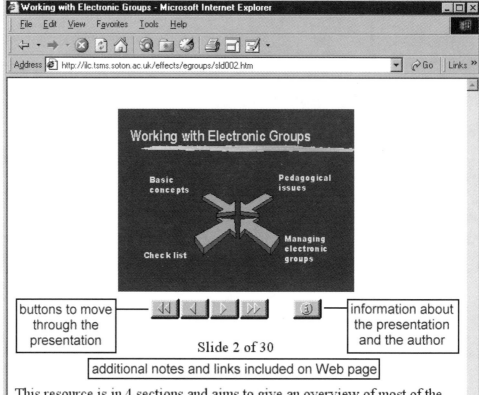

Figure 2.4 *A Microsoft PowerPoint presentation saved for use on the Web*

- An OHP and printed OHTs. You will need these even if you are planning to present using a computer, just in case the technology lets you down.
- A data projector or LCD tablet if you are going to present using a computer.
- A photocopier to duplicate your handouts.

Presenting using a computer

If you are thinking about presenting using a computer, you will need to carefully balance the benefits and costs. If all the equipment is ready to go and you are familiar with the room and the technology – great! On the other hand, if you have to book the equipment and set it up at the start of the talk, it will have to offer real educational benefits to be worthwhile. Do remember that you will still always need an OHP and printed OHTs available as a backup if something goes wrong. Here are some suggestions:

- If you choose to present via a computer, you need to be confident that the equipment works, that your presentation appears as planned and that you know how to use the software. Allow extra time to check everything before the event, and about five minutes at the start to get the equipment plugged in and the presentation loaded.
- If you have your own portable PC, or a departmental one, you can copy your presentation to it and check it before the event. Otherwise you will need to copy your presentation to the PC at the venue. Simple presentations will fit on a floppy disk, but adding multimedia will soon exceed the 1.4 MB available. Your best options are to write the presentation on to a CD ROM, if you have a CD writer, or to transfer the file across the institution's network, assuming the venue's PC is connected to it. You may need to ask for technical assistance the first couple of times you attempt this! If neither of these options is available you will need to think again – perhaps try to borrow a portable PC for the day. For regular use, your own portable PC is the only sensible option.
- Very small groups can cluster round the computer's screen, but most groups will need it projected on to a big screen so they can all read it.
  - *Data projectors* are expensive, but produce a sharp, colourful image. They can also be used to project TV and video. Older projectors sometimes have problems displaying the output from PCs. You need to check before the event that the PC and projector work together, that you have all the right leads and know where to plug them in.
  - *Liquid Crystal Display (LCD)* tablets are flat display panels that sit on top of an OHP and plug in to your PC. Again, you need to check before the event that the PC and LCD tablet work together, that you have all the right leads and know where to plug them in. The image produced may only be black and white and is not as bright or clear. The OHP should have a powerful 400-watt bulb, otherwise the image will be dim and more difficult to read. LCD tablets are generally unsuitable for use with video.
- Brightly lit rooms make the projected image difficult to see, although modern data projectors are often acceptable in normally lit rooms. You may need to draw the blinds or dim the room lights, especially with LCD tablets. Make sure that your slides have dark text on a plain pale background if this is likely to be a problem.

● If you choose to use digitized video in your presentations you will need to be aware of the limitations of the technology you use. (See section 2.3.7 on digital video.)

Comments

You can use presentation software to create posters for exhibitions and conferences. You will need to find out if your institution's printing services can print out large posters for conferences from your file. You will also want to check the cost before you do any work – large printed posters can be expensive. Alternatively, A3 colour inkjet printers are relatively cheap and can produce impressive results. The output should be laminated (enclosed in a thin transparent plastic film) to protect it and make it look glossy – ask your printing service about this inexpensive treatment.

Keep your presentation material clear and simple with not too much text. The more text you have on your OHP, the more students will just copy what you've written. The less you have, the more they have to synthesize what you say in order to make notes. Your slides should offer the structure for their note-taking, possibly based on printed hand-outs. Creating good presentations is more than just a technical skill – see the Active*Guide for advice on good design and oral presentation skills.

It is quite useful for your students to learn how to use a presentation program for group presentations as well as creating posters for assignments.

Lecturing with WWW – Physiology and Biophysics

http://galileo.physiology.uiowa.edu/lectures/

2.3.3 Digital images

■ ■ ❑ ❑ ❑

Many tutors use a personal collection of slides in their teaching. Too often the students can only see those images for a few minutes before they are returned to the filing cabinet. Technically, it is relatively simple to digitize the images and make them available on the Web so that they can be viewed whenever the students wish. In addition, the tutor can create assignments based around the use and analysis of images – this is a powerful technique in most disciplines, especially since it doesn't rely on access to specific books.

Slides or negatives are inexpensive to digitize – currently around 45p per negative or 70p per slide. Most high street photographic shops can provide this service. Your pictures will be stored as high-quality image files on a CD ROM disk. You will need to use image-editing software to create lower-quality copies of these files to include in word-processed documents, presentations or Web pages.

Photographic prints can be digitized using a scanner. These low-cost devices look like a tiny photocopier and plug in to your PC. They come with image-editing software that acts like a digital darkroom so you can change the brightness and colour balance, remove unwanted details (such as 'red-eye' from flash photos) and add text if needed.

Scanners can also digitize printed images from books or magazines, although you should be aware of the copyright restrictions detailed in section 2.4.

If you want to avoid scanning, you could use a digital camera to take any photos needed. The quality of modern digital cameras is more than acceptable for the uses discussed and they have the advantage of no film or developing costs. The image files are usually stored on special memory cards that plug in to the camera, but these are expensive and can only hold a few high-quality images. In the near future, miniature disk drives will allow hundreds of high-quality images to be stored. The images are downloaded from the camera to your PC via a special cable for more permanent storage.

The main disadvantage of digital cameras is their reliance on batteries and the speed at which they exhaust them, so take plenty of spares if you are using one on a field trip. You will also need a laptop PC to download your pictures and make room on the camera's memory card for new ones. A second disadvantage is the puny flash units built in to most digital cameras; only the most expensive models have a connector that allows a powerful external flash gun to be used.

Advantages

- A CD ROM is a safe way to store a selection of slides.
- Scanners can be used to acquire images from many sources.
- You can include your images in documents, presentations or posters created using software like Microsoft Word or PowerPoint.
- You can include your images on Web pages.

Disadvantages

- A CD ROM is an archive medium, so if your pictures or images are time sensitive this isn't an ideal choice.
- Accessing large, high-quality images using the Internet via a modem and phone line can be very slow. It is a good idea to use 'thumbnail images' (a small version of your picture) that act as a link to the large picture. Your students can then decide if they want to look at any particular picture in detail. See the Active*Guide to find out how to do this.

Equipment required

- A digital camera if you wish to take your own digital photographs.
- A scanner if you wish to digitize photographic prints, books or printed images.

Comments

You will need to be systematic in the way you name your image files and store them in folders. Some image-editing software comes with browser software that shows you thumbnail versions of every image in a directory, so you can find and choose images visually.

Digital images, or bitmaps, are a grid of coloured dots, like a computer screen or TV picture. When seen from a distance, the dots blend into a photo-realistic picture. These dots are usually known as 'pixels'.

The quality of the picture largely depends on the *resolution* of the image – the width and height of the picture measured in pixels. The more pixels that are used, the finer the detail that can be shown. However, the higher the resolution, the larger the computer file needed to store the colour data for all the pixels.

The second factor affecting image quality is the *colour depth:* the range of possible colours for each pixel. This is determined by the number of bits of data used to encode the colour. Most digital images use 24 bits of data per pixel, which allows around 16 million colours. All these colours allow the subtle shading and variation in hue present in photographs to be accurately captured and stored.

Digital image files can be very large: a full-page photo printed in a magazine might easily be 20 megabytes or more. The size of the file can be reduced by storing it in a *compressed* file format which relies on complex mathematical techniques to discard information that your eye doesn't notice and encode the remaining data efficiently. In general, photographs can be compressed to 10 per cent of their original size with little loss in image quality. In any case, the level of compression applied can be adjusted to match the quality required. For some images in which accurate detail is essential, such as x-rays, compression is inappropriate.

The Web uses two image file formats: GIF (pronounced with a hard 'g' as in girl) and JPEG (pronounced 'jay-peg'). GIFs are used for all types of small graphics while JPEGs are used for photographs. Both formats use compression to make the files as small as possible and minimize the time taken to transfer them across the Internet.

Painting software is available that produces the same type of files as scanned digital images, except that you need a good deal of artistic skill to 'paint' an image from scratch. Most image-editing software includes painting tools so that you can retouch scanned images.

You can buy clip-art CDs containing copyright-free images. Typically these hold around 100 high-quality professional photographs based on a theme (eg, African Birds) at a reasonable price. These may be an excellent resource if you are lucky enough to find a CD that covers the topic you need.

Channel MarketMakers

http://www.cmm1.com/

They sell over 700 low-cost Corel PhotoCDs, each with 100 images. You can view thumbnails of the images on each CD to see if they match your needs.

Creating Interactive PhotoCDs

Bob Lister: paper presented at the 1998 Humanities and Arts Higher Education Network's Conference

http://www-iet.open.ac.uk/iet/herg/BobLister-HANconf98.html

Abstract: The aim of this paper is to show how the computer can maximize the potential of visual resources for both the teacher and the learner. Drawing on examples of best practice provided by existing photo-CDs in the field of Classics, this paper will look at issues involved in developing visual resources for multiple audiences.

2.3.4   Graphics and clip-art

■ ■ ■ ❑ ❑

Why explain something in words when a diagram can convey it much more succinctly? Diagrams can provide an overview at a glance and show linkages, relationships and processes.

Graphics are drawings, diagrams, charts and graphs that have been created using computer software. This is distinct from the digitized images discussed in section 2.3.3, which are derived from photographs or printed images.

Advantages

- Drawing software enables you to create and edit graphics with the same ease as a word-processor does with documents. It provides tools that make it simple to add, edit, move, copy and align shapes such as rectangles, circles, lines, arrows and text.

- Drawings can easily be included in word-processed documents or presentations, or saved as images for use on Web pages.

- Most presentation software includes a useful set of drawing tools, so you may not need to buy and learn new software.

- Spreadsheets can be used to automatically create charts and graphs based on specified data. These charts can easily be included in word-processed documents or presentations, or saved as images for use on Web pages.

Disadvantages

- A good deal of skill and experience is needed to create realistic or complex graphics – the learning curve for some software is quite steep.

Equipment required

- Drawing software.

- A laser printer or colour inkjet printer if you need printed copies or OHTs.

Comments

'Clip-art' is a term used to describe collections of drawings or images that can be freely used in your documents, presentations and Web sites without any copyright payments or restrictions. You can buy low-cost CDs containing tens of thousands of pieces of clip-art, covering all types of subject. Presentation and drawing software often comes with a CD of clip-art and vast amounts are freely available for download from the Internet. The main problem with it is the time taken to find the image or drawing you need.

 Free Graphics by Syruss – Free Backgrounds and Free Graphics!

http://www.syruss.com/

 Barry's Clip Art Server

http://barrysclipart.com/

 Encyclopedia of Educational Technology

Bob Hoffman (1999) San Diego State University

http://coe.sdsu.edu/eet/

Follow the 'contents' link and then select: Image Resolution and File Size Concerns in Web Page Design. This is an excellent Web site for all kinds of information on educational technology.

 Image Learning

Ben Davis (1991) presented at the Technology & Education Conference, Ekpedeftiria Doukas SA, Athens, Greece

http://www.mit.edu:8001/people/davis/ImageLearn.html

Education has reified text almost to the exclusion of other kinds of information. This article discusses how multimedia is opening the doorway to all kinds of media that we can now easily assemble and present in a learning environment.

2.3.5 Web pages

■ ■ ■ ❏ ❏

Web pages are not really a type of multimedia, but more a way of integrating many different types of media and making them available to anyone with access to the Internet.

Modern software makes creating Web pages as easy as using a word-processor. You can design your pages visually and never have to see or learn the HTML (HyperText Markup Language) code that defines their content and appearance.

Internet Explorer and Netscape Navigator come with simple editors that enable you to create Web pages visually, and these are great as learning tools. However, if you want to create a Web site containing more than 20 pages, you will need to use more sophisticated programs that are designed to help you create and manage Web sites. There are some excellent educational deals available for this type of software, so do check with your computing service what they recommend before you buy. See Active*Guide for some simple step-by-step exercises that you can use to learn how to create your first Web pages, plus guidance on more advanced topics.

These Web sites have tutorials, reference material and guidance on topics such as how to structure your Web site so it is easy to use:

 WebMonkey

http://www.webmonkey.com

If you can stand the rather gaudy colour scheme, this site has some of the best tutorials available.

 Builder.com

http://www.builder.com

This is part of the c|net empire of online technology magazines, and has terrific resources for anyone creating Web sites.

2.3.6 Digital audio

■ ■ ❑ ❑ ❑

There are many disciplines in which a sound clip can be a useful teaching aid. Examples include:

- Selected examples of contemporary advertising in business, management, media studies or social sciences.
- Extracts from historical speeches in politics, history or social sciences.
- Authors' readings of poetry or literature.
- Recordings of healthy and abnormal heart sounds in medicine.
- Recordings of engine noise or vibration in engineering.

Modern software makes it very easy to create digital sound files from original recordings on tape or CD. Recordings from vinyl records, radio, TV or a microphone are best stored on tape first. Good quality cassette tape is one option, or use DAT (digital audio tape) for the highest quality.

You will need to understand how the copyright laws affect taking clips from broadcast or pre-recorded sources – in most cases it is illegal unless you gain written permission from the copyright holder, possibly by paying a licence fee. See section 2.4 for more information.

Advantages
- The sound clip can be carefully selected and edited so it only contains the material required.
- The sound clip can easily be replayed if required, for example to assist in comparing two clips.

- The sound clip can be made available on the Web for further study and revision by the students.

Disadvantages

- If the sound clip is part of a multimedia presentation, the venue will have to have suitable amplification and speakers connected to the PC used. The speakers commonly available with PCs are inadequate for anything but small groups. The PC will also have to have a sound card.
- If the sound clip is available on the Web, the PCs used by the students will need a sound card installed and either speakers or headphones. You may find that most if not all of these PCs lack these, since they lead to either noisy computer rooms or stolen headphones.
- Sound files can get quite large and may not fit on a floppy disk. You will need a CD writer, ZIP drive (or similar) or server to back up or transfer files.

Equipment required

- Suitable PC with sound card and speakers or headphones.
- Tape recorder with suitable input and output sockets. You may also need a microphone.
- Leads to connect the tape recorder to the PC's sound card and to any audio sources used.
- Software to digitize sound – this often comes with the sound card. Simple software is also provided as standard with both Windows and MacOS.

Comments

Check that the computers available to your students can play sound files before you plan to make use of audio resources – try this out with a sample file. It is usually impractical to have speakers for each computer (think of the noise!) so headphones are often the preferred option. Students may have to provide and plug in their own headphones if they want to listen to sound.

Unfortunately, many appropriate uses of sound clips are prevented by the difficulty and cost of obtaining copyright clearance. However, for disciplines like ancient or modern languages, music or medicine, where 'home-made' recordings can be digitized, there are many opportunities for their creative use in supporting learning.

2.3.7   Digital video

■ ■ ■ ■ ❑

Video clips can be digitized, stored as highly compressed files, distributed using LANs or the Internet and displayed on modern computers. The quality ranges from poor (small windows, jerky movement) to very good (full screen, smooth motion) depending on the type of digital video and the power of the computer used to view it.

Digital video delivered using the Internet is best suited to short video clips that can be selected and played 'on demand'. Students can view these clips again and again if needed. High-quality, full-screen video requires distribution via fast LAN networks or on CD ROM.

Advantages

- Dangerous or expensive experiments can be demonstrated. The video can also highlight common mistakes and show what happens if things go wrong.
- The equipment and procedures used in practical sessions and field work can be demonstrated to prepare students in advance and make the best use of their time.
- Additional video material can be used to illustrate a point. You may need professional help to edit your material, although modern software makes this a relatively easy process.
- Case studies of clients can be presented. You have several options here:
  - you film 'clients' or 'patients' with their consent for this to be used educationally (if you want this to be a commercial product, you will need further clearance from those involved);
  - you film as above with permissions, but may wish to make the person anonymous by disguising the face;
  - you find an actor to do this for you. You could take the transcript from a real case (as long as the text is anonymous).
- Students can use video to record field trips or experiments.

Disadvantages

- Video is an archive medium and cannot be changed, so it is less useful for material that will date quickly.
- The cost of making a video may be high – especially if you use actors.
- Creating and using digital video requires a lot of technical expertise, although modern software and hardware are demystifying and simplifying the process.

Equipment required

- A video source – either a camcorder or a video player. Note that digitizing prerecorded or broadcast programmes will require written copyright clearance in all cases; see section 2.4.
- A suitable Windows PC or Apple Mac that has inputs that you can plug the video source into. Low-cost digitizing cards are available if your PC needs upgrading. Note that your PC will need a fast, modern processor, lots of memory and a large hard disk for good results. You will also need a CD writer to conveniently archive the huge digital video files.

● Digital video editing software. This usually comes free with the digitizing hardware, although you may want to upgrade to another program that provides more features or greater ease of use.

● Digital video recorders are now available and these can be linked directly to computers that have a suitable socket. The advantage of these is that the video is already digital and does not need to be encoded before it can be edited, which results in higher quality and greater ease of use.

Digital video standards

There are several standards for digital video that you will need to choose from. Some of these support *progressive download*, which means the video file starts to play after a few seconds, but will pause if the data download speed cannot keep up. The use of special Web server software allows true streaming, in which the quality of the video is continually adjusted to match the download speed to avoid any pauses.

Windows AVI is an obsolete format that can only be played on Windows PCs and has large files that give a small, low-quality video window. Don't use this.

Apple QuickTime can be used on both Windows and Mac computers that have the free QuickTime player installed. It is commonly used in multimedia applications since it integrates well with the software used to create them. QuickTime is also widely used for putting digital video on the Web, delivered via progressive download or true streaming if a dedicated media server is used. QuickTime supports many media types, including audio, video, text, MPEG, MIDI, QuickTime VR panoramas and 3D.

Windows Media Technologies is Microsoft's streaming media system, designed to deliver video and audio across networks to Windows 95/98 and Apple Mac computers that have the free player installed. It offers limited support for progressive download as well as true streaming if a Windows Media Server is used.

RealSystem G2, also known as *RealAudio* and *RealVideo*, is a true streaming media system developed by RealNetworks. It delivers video and audio across the Web to Windows 95/98 and Apple Mac computers that have the free player installed. Free software is available to encode video and audio, while more advanced 'Pro' versions are available at a price. Other low-cost software enables multimedia presentations to be put together easily, including PowerPoint with a voice-over.

MPEG is a digital file format developed by the Moving Picture Experts Group (MPEG) to handle video and audio. The disadvantage of this format is that the whole file must be downloaded before it starts to play.

The low bandwidth (data speed) of home Internet connections means that digital video usually appears in a small window. However, if high bandwidth is available using a LAN or CD ROM, then QuickTime, Windows Media Technologies and MPEG can all deliver full-screen, full-motion VHS-quality video and sound.

Comments

Is the digital video to be used in a lecture or as a self-study resource? If it is in a lecture, you will need a suitable PC and a data projector. The video file will have to be stored on a CD ROM or accessed via a high-speed network connection. If it is self-study, do students have adequate access to suitable computers that can be used to view the video resources?

Short video clips can be used in lectures to illustrate processes, procedures, case studies, artefacts, places or historical events. They are not ideal to present a 'talking head' since you could summarize those points better yourself. Think carefully about the educational purpose of the clip.

Self-study video resources should be short and to the point – edit out unnecessary material. Break longer clips into chunks so that specific sections can be accessed and linked.

You could video your lecture so students can have flexible access to this resource and weaker students have the chance of viewing it several times. Video tape may be a better option than digital video, but you will need multiple copies for loan.

If you intend the video to replace real lectures, bear in mind that it is a very passive learning resource that is unlikely to be effective or popular. How will it compare to TV programmes on science, nature or history that have very high production values?

 Desktop Video World

http://idiots-guide.matroxusers.com/

A good introduction to the practicalities, including advice on hardware, software, the process and frequently asked questions.

 Codec Central

http://www.terran.com/CodecCentral/index.html

A one-stop source for information on digital video technologies that includes articles that lead you through the process of creating high-quality digital video.

 Apple QuickTime

http://www.apple.com/quicktime/

Download the free player, view and listen to sample files and find out more.

 Windows Media Technologies

http://www.microsoft.com/windows/windowsmedia/en/default.asp

Download the free player, view and listen to sample files and find out more.

RealNetworks

http://www.real.com

Download the free player and encoder software, view and listen to sample files and find out more.

MPEG.ORG

http://www.mpeg.org/MPEG/

Links to software and other resources plus all the information you need.

2.3.8 Simulations

■ ■ ■ ■ ■

Simulations are an excellent learning tool for all aspects of education, but particularly in areas such as medicine, management, science and engineering, which make extensive use of case studies and systems that can be modelled mathematically.

There is a close association between modelling, case studies and simulations. Models represent structures, whereas simulations reflect the process of interactions between the structures when certain parameters are manipulated, causing a change in behaviour. With that definition, case studies can be a simulation if there is an observable effect on the 'case' as a result of the student's behaviour (or lack of it). Simulations are wide-ranging, showing the change over time within mathematical, cognitive, physical, computer and social models.

Advantages

- Excellent learning tool to encourage deep learning.
- Computer-based simulations can be used in lectures and tutorials or for self-study by students – in both cases they allow active experimentation with ideas.

Disadvantages

- It is difficult to make your own simulations, even using special-purpose software. You will need to learn programming and to express the simulation structure and rules in a precise and logical way.
- Creating simulations can be very time-consuming – they need extensive testing to ensure they behave correctly in all situations.
- Simulations can be rather slow when used over the Internet, so delivery on a CD ROM may be a better option in some cases.

Equipment required

- A powerful PC or Mac to run interactive simulations.
- If you purchase simulations, check carefully the kind of computer you need. You may find that it only runs on UNIX computers, for example.
- If you want to run the simulation across the network, check the implications of this with your computing services. Check speed of access using the network. If sound is used, will students be provided with headphones, will they bring their own, or can they hire them?

- Software such as Stella Modelling Software and the Multiverse Simulation Environment is designed to help you produce your own simulations. Conventional multimedia software such as Macromedia Director and ToolBook can also be used.

- If you are a competent programmer, you can create simulations using languages such as Visual Basic, C++ or Java. The latter has the advantage that it can easily be delivered across the Web.

Comments

Creating your own simulation will take a good deal of effort, time and expertise. You should check before you start in case someone else has already produced one that fits your needs. This is particularly true of small Java 'applets' (programs) that provide interactive simulations of common topics in science and engineering – check the links given below for searchable archives containing hundreds of these small programs. You should also check the Mailbase 'simulations' list for news of suitable simulations by first searching their archive of messages and then posting a request.

Simulations-for-education (mailbase, discussion facility)

http://www.mailbase.ac.uk

Select 'S' from the menu and search until you find the correct discussion group.

Educational Resources at Gamelan.com

http://www.gamelan.com/directories/pages/dir.java.educational.html

Lists over 1300 Java applets that can be downloaded and used in courses. Many are shareware and request a modest fee for use. Mostly cover maths, engineering and science, with some languages and medicine.

Physics and Astronomy Applets

http://jersey.uoregon.edu/vlab/

Interactive Java curriculum modules from the University of Oregon Physics Department. Topics include mechanics, energy, thermodynamics and astrophysics.

Stella Modelling Software

http://www.hps-inc.com/edu/index.htm

Stella, A Simulation Construction Kit; Cognitive Processes and Educational Implications

Marlo Steed, University of Lethbridge, Faculty of Education, Canada

http://www.edu.uleth.ca/faculty/members/steed/Stella/Stella.html

Multiverse Simulation Environment

http://www.ltc.hw.ac.uk/mverse/old/

This is a new company based at Heriot-Watt University, offering bespoke simulations to higher education. It is open to discuss any of your requirements for simulation use in learning and teaching. It has developed a product for handling simulations which is currently free to UK higher education and can be obtained from its Web site.

Macromedia Director (support and developers centre)

http://www.macromedia.com/support/director/downloads.html

Comments

Simulations are good for testing theories, observing results and experimenting with ideas. Simulations are a good example of experiential and constructivist learning, ie learning that is achieved by student manipulation. Students therefore 'construct' their own learning. Simulations are also good for looking at the dynamics of a process or system and investigating the results of manipulating parameters. Simulations are an excellent 'thinking' tool.

Simulations are a simplified representation of the dynamics of a process – if there are too many inter-linked variables, the students will simply become confused.

Make sure the students can see the effects of their decisions or changes on the process being studied. What is the follow-up work to the simulation? How can they apply what they have learnt?

Below are some sites you can visit to see some simulations in action.

Virtual Hospital – Patient simulations (more like case studies)

http://www.vh.org/Providers/Simulations/PatientSimulations.html

Case studies here are free to look at.

MedSim: Advanced Medical Simulations

http://www.medsim.com/

This is a commercial company, but there are some demos for viewing.

Educational Space Simulations Project

http://chico.rice.edu/armadillo/Simulations/simserver.html

A good deal of information on space simulation with links to meteorology, weather and climate sites, NASA's online educational resources, planetariums on the Net, etc.

Electrophysiology

http://pb010.anes.ucla.edu/

The site has some good interactive simulations.

Simulations and Animations

http://www.astro.ubc.ca/~scharein/a311/Sim.html#Doppler

Good demonstrations of using small programs (applets) for 'the big bang', 'fusion of the sun', Doppler effect, etc. They are designed to allow some small changes in the model and you can observe the effect.

Computer-based Simulations and CYMAP

http://ctiweb.cf.ac.uk/HABITAT/HABITAT4/cymap.htm

School of the Built Environment, University of Ulster at Jordanstown

2.4   Copyright issues

If you decide to go ahead with a resource base that comprises material (text, pictures, video, etc) from others, you will need to seriously consider the copyright implications. This is by no means straightforward, and this section summarizes the issues involved.

What is covered by copyright?

The answer to this is virtually everything, but the essence is 'a creative work'. As soon as an author commits his or her creative thoughts into a tangible form, be that film, painting, World Wide Web, sculpture, prose, etc, then they are covered by copyright, by default, even if there is no copyright mark to say so. The copyright mark, ©, however, is usually inserted to avoid any ambiguity. The correct way to indicate copyright is:

© (author/owner), (date/s)

Nine different types of work are protected by copyright:

1. Literary works (including letters, memos, directories, song lyrics, computer programs, computer codes).
2. Dramatic works (including stage directions, instructions for dance and mime).
3. Musical works (scores, directions).
4. Artistic works (including photographs, sculptures, some architecture and artistic craftsmanship).
5. Sound recordings.
6. Films.
7. Broadcasts (including satellite).
8. Cable programmes.
9. Published editions (including layout and typography).

In addition, there are performers' rights, which are relevant to several of the types of work listed above (for instance, films, broadcasts and sound recordings).

Frequently asked questions about copyright
If it is in the public domain can I use it?

This may mean that the author has given up the rights of that work for anyone to use.

However, you cannot assume that, and it is your responsibility (and courtesy) to clear this with the author. Don't forget we all have copyright for our creative thoughts by default.

If I use it for education and don't charge for it, is it alright?

Basically, no. There is a 'fair dealing' clause that allows educators a *small* allowance. You may have heard that copying less than 10 per cent of a work is permissible, but this is not true. It is not so much the quantity as the quality of what is copied. If, for example, taking 2 per cent of someone's work rendered the remainder of their work useless, then this would infringe copyright. Determining the percentage of the work permissible, therefore, is quite difficult. You can of course use referenced quotes from other authors for review purposes.

If there is no copyright statement on the work, can I use it freely?

No. We must seek permission for use of all creative work. Our work is by default our copyright unless we sell that right, or agree beforehand that it belongs to those who have paid us to carry out the work.

Does this mean I can't supply other authors' work to my students?

The copyright law protects authors' rights to the commercial benefits of their work and the right to control that work. Usually if you ask the authors' permission (assuming they have the copyright and not someone else) they will be only too glad to help out. Make sure you clear the extent of the copyright. Is it for your class only, for campus-wide delivery, for an international group of students, etc?

How do I get copyright clearance?

In seeking copyright clearance for each of these, you need to be clear about who owns the copyright and what the terms of the copyright are. You then need to contact the owner of the copyright, or 'collecting societies' who act on behalf of copyright owners, explaining how you intend to use the material.

The terms of copyright on different types of work vary considerably, and are influenced by different copyright laws, the main ones being the 1911 Act, the 1956 Act and the 1988 Act. Terms vary: 25 years for published editions, the author's life, or 70 years after his or her death for literary works.

Once you have established who owns the copyright, you need to contact the owner to ask permission to use the material, giving the following information:

- The title of the new work, and its aims.
- A description of the target audience.
- A description of how it will be distributed (ie, commercially or not for profit) and the geographical coverage of the expected marketing.
- The name of the publisher/distributor dealing with the new work.

Tracking down the individual copyright owner is often difficult. It is worth starting by contacting the most relevant 'collecting society' to see if the copyright owner is registered there. If so, the staff can advise you about terms and conditions of use, and payment where this is required. If the work is on the World Wide Web, then there is usually a Web address where you can contact the author. You can also simply search an author's name on the Web and invariably come up with an e-mail address. Some of the collecting societies are:

British Phonographic Industry http://www.bpi.co.uk/corporat.htm
Christian Copyright Licensing http://www.ccli.com/(international site)
Design and Artistic Copyright Society
International Federation of Phonographic Industries
Mechanical Copyright Protection Society
The Ordnance Survey http://www.davidmorgan.com/CATALOGS/DM/dm39
Performing Rights Society
Phonographic Performance Ltd
Video Performance Ltd

For further information about these and other collecting societies, contact the Copyright Licensing Agency.

Remember the onus is on you to obtain copyright clearance. Reference your resources meticulously so you can trace ownership easily. Be clear what you want copyright clearance for: limited or worldwide market? Can you protect your World Wide Web site for use only with local students? Each time you broaden the reach of your work, you will need to get new clearance.

Copyright Licensing Agency (CLA)

http://www.cla.co.uk/

CLA is responsible for looking after the interests of copyright owners in copying from books, journals and periodicals. This is an excellent site for all kinds of information on copyright (internationally). It also has a section on higher education.

Shifting Boundaries of Intellectual Property: Copyright, Intellectual Property, and Publishing on the WWW

Jeffrey R Galin (1998) University of Pittsburgh

http://www.pitt.edu/~hypertch/copyright.html

This is an excellent 'all round' site for copyright issues connected with the Web.

ACTIVITY 2E

Checklist for Chapter 2

Consider the following before you create multimedia resources (assets):

1. Do you and your students meet the requirements covering computer access, skills and support outlined in section 2.2?

2. If you want to use multimedia resources, have you searched to see if you can get these resources already in a digital format? You can try the subject-specific resource gateways on the Web and the Learning & Teaching Support Network in the UK (see section 1.3.3) and relevant mailbases (http://www.mailbase.ac.uk).

3. Do you know what to do with your resources once they are digitized – technically (see section 2.3) and pedagogically? How will you use this multimedia resource to enhance learning? See also Chapter 3 for a more detailed discussion on designing learning environments.

4. Have you checked copyright issues of using resources prepared by others? See section 2.4.

5. Is the resource you want to digitize text, images, audio or video? Do you know which software packages you will need? Do you know how to do this, or can you get help?

6. If you go ahead on your own and get suitable software, have you checked that your institution can support you with this software? Have you checked the licensing arrangement of any software you will use? Check that it is suitable for multiple users.

References

Cross, P K (1995) *Teaching and Learning in the Next Century*, http://www.ntlf. com/html/sf/teaching.htm

England, E and Finney, A (1999) *Managing Multimedia: Project Management for Interactive Media*, 2nd edn, Addison-Wesley, Harlow (Chapter 14 on video asset production, Chapter 15 on graphic asset production. These give you more professional information.)

Gibbs, G (1992) 'Independent learning with more students', in *Teaching More Students Project*, Oxford Centre for Staff Development, Oxford

Min, F B M (1992) 'Parallel instruction: a theory for educational computer simulation', *Interactive Learning International*, **8**, pp 177–83

3 Designing learning environments

In this chapter we will discuss the role that open learning materials play in the independent learning arena, and how these can be developed via resource-based learning. Open learning here is taken to mean an instructional method that encompasses a variety of resources designed to be used by students independently of the tutor. We refer to resource-based learning as the crafting of a wide variety of resources into a coherent open learning environment. It can include, for example, work-alone paper-based tutorials with exercises, and group work involving problem solving and case-based learning. Computer technology is now playing a vital role in this area of education. Computers can be used to prepare, compile and deliver educational material – in fact offer integrated access to multimedia open learning environments.

In order to prepare good open learning environments, whether open learning packs or online learning environments, we need to seriously think about the design of our course. For example, is our style of teaching congruent with our values and philosophy for the course, and do the resources enable the students to achieve the learning outcomes effectively? In this chapter we will discuss:

- the different kinds of open learning materials (section 3.1);
- independent learning and its role in open learning (section 3.2);
- how to plan and design resource bases for open learning environments (section 3.3).

This chapter introduces the technological tools to help you do this and some practical exercises to try out through the Active*Guide on the Web site, http://www.clt.soton. ac.uk/activeguide.

3.1 Open learning materials

Learning packs are one kind of open learning environment and designed to support students in independent study. They need to be written in a way that takes the student fairly painlessly through the resources, balancing challenging material with limited frustration.

Learning packs are traditionally seen as readers with exercises or assignments, as in the early UK Open University materials. They can also be more structured and based on guided tutorials that encourage reader interactivity with a variety of exercises spread throughout the material. The material can comprise print, audio and video tapes,

Table 3.1 *Types of open learning materials*

Learning Pack	Description	Advantages
Learning packages	Full student notes with exercises/concepts that students need to be familar with before the lecture	Lectures can focus on problem areas, additional material and overviews. It may even be possible to dispense with some lecture sessions
Readers/Study Guides	Core textual material that is difficult to obtain, eg chapters from books and articles. These may be accompanied by commentaries, questions, summaries and seminar topics as well as further reading lists	Ensure that everyone has access to key texts so that all students can be prepared for seminars. They also structure the topic, giving students a framework for their own research
Laboratory/Field Journals	A short description of each 'activity' (experiment/field work) with information on: ■ Procedural instructions ■ Analysis methods ■ Relation to theory ■ Report writing techniques ■ Reading lists See also manuals and guides	Students may be able to carry out their work without an academic member of staff being present. Technical staff can provide equipment needed
Manuals and Guides	Used for equipment, instruments, computer-based learning packages, project work, dissertations, safety regulations	Equipment and instrument manuals could be held at suitable access points for use when necessary
Course Guides	These contain: ■ Course aims/rationale ■ Learning outcomes ■ Timetable ■ Key texts ■ Commentaries ■ Seminar titles/expected performance ■ Methods of assessment ■ Assignments ■ Additional media such as PCs, audio, video ■ Reading lists	These prepare the student for the breadth of the course. He or she is aware of what is expected from day one. Many non-essential face-to-face sessions can be dispensed with

Source: Gibbs, 'Designing Learning Packages: Module 8', in *Teaching in Higher Education by Open Learning*

photographs, television, radio, computer packages, equipment and various other artefacts. These are traditionally used in distance learning, but with increasing student numbers and a need for more independent flexible learning methods, they can be a useful resource for full- or part-time students.

Open learning material need not necessarily be complex. Some intermediary open learning material is shown in Table 3.1

ACTIVITY 3A

What material do you use in support of a lecture course?

	Regularly	Sometimes	Never
Course guides			
Lecture notes (handed out each week)			
Lecture packages			
Readers/study guides			
Reading lists			
Problem solving exercises/case studies			
Laboratory/field journals			
Instructions for coursework, laboratory, field work (handed out each week)			
Manuals			
Word-processed material			
Material saved at 'html' (hyptertext mark up language) ready for Web delivery			

Feedback

If you have answered 'regularly' or 'sometimes' to most of these and if they have been word-processed, then you are well on your way to producing a complete learning package. The effort needed to move to more independent learning materials is therefore reduced.

If you said 'never' to having converted any of your material to HTML, then consult the Active*Guide Web site.

3.2 Key considerations when writing open learning materials

Learning packs can be unpopular with full-time students if they completely replace tutors and/or are badly written. When open learning materials are used with full- or part-time students, it should be made clear that the material is there to support their learning and encourage independence. However, the tutor must not 'withdraw' completely and students should be allowed access times to the tutor or postgraduate teaching assistants as part of their support mechanism. It may also be wise to set up peer-assisted learning groups that encourage cooperation between students. This could be a good preparation for more collaborative learning assignments you may set them later, as well as developing the key skill 'working with others'.

They should be encouraged to give feedback on the value of the material and suggest improvements. Third-year students could even opt to rewrite some sections, or additional sections as part of a project. Also, arrange sufficient communication (either face-to-face or electronic) with and between your students so they feel part of a learning community – after all, they elected for full-time study and this is an essential part of it (see section 4.1.3).

Components of open learning environments are, according to Reigeluth (1999):

Enabling contexts	The opportunities and restrictions (internal or external) that shape decisions (see activity 3B below) eg, accessibility to computers.
Resources	These include tutors, peers, library, electronic resources that can provide the needed information.
Tools	Means of engaging and manipulating both resources and ideas.
Scaffolding	The processes that support individual learning efforts such as: conceptual – what to consider; metacognitive – ways of thinking; procedural – the rubric; strategic – methods of approach.

The *scaffolding* is how you set up the learning material to enhance learning. Decide the kind of scaffolding you want to provide in your learning environments. Conceptual scaffolding will focus the student on a particular aspect of the problem. This can take the form of providing tools for the task, giving prompts and hints (implicit or explicit), concept maps, etc. Metacognitive scaffolding will guide the student in *how* to think about a particular problem/study. Particular strategies will be encouraged that are consonant with a field of study. Study skills can be used here in terms of planning, developing objectivity, being rigorous, etc. Once this is developed, it should be a self-regulatory process. Procedural scaffolding guides students in using the learning material, how to find more resources, how to use the system and help files in computer aided learning packages, etc. Strategic scaffolding will guide the student towards effective analysis, planning and tactical decision making. Students will be able to identify and evaluate new information and relate this to existing knowledge. This can be encouraged through probing questions that give strategic clues, a set of related questions on-demand that further test the students' understanding of the topic/problem and extend their horizons (Hannafin *et al*, 1999).

Traditionally, open learning materials have focused on the syllabus, ie the content. However, with the shift towards more independent learning, process skills, especially in terms of group work, are becoming increasingly important. The following section looks at some methods of group work we could put into practice.

3.2.1 Methods of teaching and modes of learning to encourage independent learning

We can encourage independent learning in the way we set up and manage our teaching. The changes we are seeing in instructional design reflect the changes we are seeing in society – see section 1.1. The focus is on meeting the learner's needs and on active learning; it is learner-centred. Instructional designers, traditionally very cognitively based, now include other types of learning such as the affective (emotional) domain, which refers, on the whole, to our interpersonal skills. (See section 5.2.1 for more information on the 'cognitive domain'.)

ACTIVITY 3B

Instructional design: where do you stand?

Have a particular course/unit in mind – maybe one that is causing you some difficulty.

Look at Figure 3.1 and mark in one colour where you think your current course/unit is, and in another colour where you would like it to be.

If there are differences, consider how you are going to move from the actual to the desired. What are the opportunities and constraints? What resources would you need? How would these changes affect your 'scaffolding', ie, the processes that support student learning?

Below are some of the strategies that we can use to encourage independent learning. For a discussion on assessing this approach, see Chapter 5.

Case-based learning/reasoning

Case-based learning is an ideal way to encapsulate experience and represent it in a 'story-like' manner. Cases should be selected that are: a) historically important, or b) unusual (the case that breaks that rule/law), or c) paradigmatic (represents a class of thing). Case-based learning helps us remember concepts, events and processes and provides a convenient mental 'label' for recalling these principles (Riesbeck and Schank, 1989).

Case studies are also used to encapsulate ideas and experiences that have been learnt. They are used very much in strategic domains, such as law, engineering, health, social work and education. Here case-based learning is used in an inductive mode where students determine, from the cases presented, the underlying principles and make the relevant decisions where the scenario calls for it.

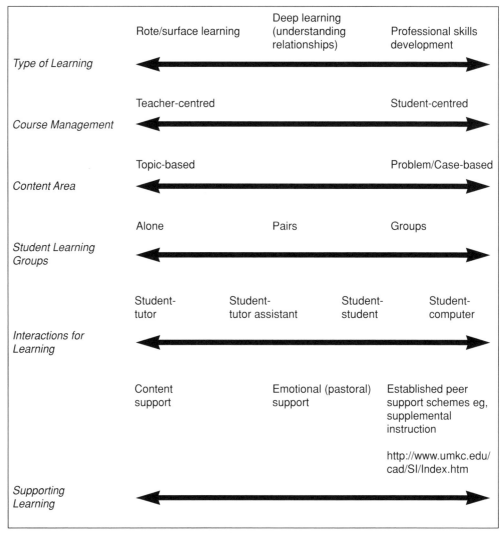

Figure 3.1 *Organizational strategies for instructional design*

Adapted from Reiugeluth, 1999

In open learning

It is excellent to use the case or story format to introduce concepts that are to appear in a section. These can be used as *advance organizers*, ie preparing students for the content to follow and as a good aid for remembering the contents of the section. Case studies can be used to consolidate learning by allowing students to utilize their newly learnt knowledge in a given case. This is ideal for individual or group work. (See section 5.3.2 'Assessing collaborative learning events'.)

Engines for Education: Central issues of case-based teaching

Roger Schank and Chip Cleary (1994) Institute for the Learning Sciences, Northwestern University

http://www.ils.nwu.edu/~e_for_e/nodes/NODE-192-pg.html

 Case-based Learning

Stacey Jobling (1998) University of West Florida

http://143.88.86.98/pacee/steps/tutorial/casebasedlearning.htm

An excellent site with lots of other references.

Problem-based learning

Problem-based learning is 'learning by doing'. Problems are usually contextualized within future workplace settings, roles or creative design. They allow students the freedom to progress through free enquiry and give them the experience of overcoming confusion and frustration (ie, cognitive conflict that restructures a student's knowledge) prior to finding a solution.

From problem-based learning, students ideally will:

- engage the challenge of the problem and become self-directed (management);
- reason effectively and creatively (critical analysis);
- apply all appropriate knowledge bases to solve the problem (application of knowledge);
- recognize where they need to find more information and how to go about it (learning skills);
- collaborate with peers (interpersonal skills);
- reflect on the process in order to improve their skills (self-awareness).

As a tutor, ensure your students are equipped with a sufficient knowledge base for the problem in question and that they have had some training in the reasoning for such problems. You may want to consider conceptual scaffolding to guide the more inexperienced learner to the core of the problem. Metacognitive scaffolding strategies may be used to encourage an approach to the problem. Make sure the goals of the exercise are clear and that students know there is probably no 'right' answer. You may, however, want to determine certain criteria for the solutions. Offering differing criteria for a solution to the same problem to different groups will encourage students to approach the problem from multiple perspectives (see Boud and Feletti, 1992).

In open learning

This is ideal for an open learning environment, whether for individual or group work. Ensure students have a sufficient knowledge base to tackle the problem. Problem-based learning really does allow students to work creatively, and to their own agenda. They should have fun solving these problems. Select problems that have several possible outcomes and let the students know there is no one answer. For assessment, however, you will need to develop a set of criteria against which all solutions (and the *process* of arriving at the solution) are measured. Ensure that the students know what these are (see section 5.3.2 'Assessing collaborative learning environments').

Problem Based Learning

Southern Illinois University School of Medicine

http://www.pbli.org/

Problem-based learning in biology – with 20 examples

http://www.saltspring.com/capewest/pbl.htm

A good 'how to' site for tutors and students.

The A thru E Approach to Problem Solving in Chemistry

Dave Woodcock (1993)

http://www.ouc.bc.ca/chem/probsol/a-e_out.html

He uses Analyse, Brainstorm, Calculate, Defend, Evaluate and looks at problem solving for science students.

Both case-based and problem-based learning are the cornerstone approaches to collaborative learning. The use of group work encourages independence from the tutor, uses peers as resources and develops interactive and team building skills.

Evidence-based learning

Evidence-based learning is predominantly associated with medicine, where trainee medical practitioners learn from patients (patient case studies, clinical practice), medical knowledge (systematic research, processes – diagnoses and treatments) and the experience of other practitioners. This method is very similar to case-based reasoning.

In open learning

This kind of learning scenario is a little more difficult to manage as the student will be adding external information from clinical practice. As with case-based and problem-based learning, ensure students have the necessary knowledge base and know how to incorporate all the evidence for a given 'case'. You will need to set guidelines for them to present their 'evidence'.

Evidence-Based Medicine Resource Center

http://ebmny.org/teach.html

📖 **Mailbase**

http://www.mailbase.ac.uk

Select 'discussion lists' and search under 'E' for 'evidence-based learning'.

Competency-based learning (or capability curriculum)

Competency-based learning is essentially concerned with the development of skills. The classic example is the apprenticeship model and more recently the UK's National Vocational Qualification (NVQ). We are now seeing the emergence of this form of learning within higher education in the area of key skills, although how we embed key skills into the curriculum is far from settled in many higher education institutions. When assessing competency-based learning, we are looking at what the learners can do, together with what they know and understand at various levels of competence.

In open learning

Most of the work here is on performing a skill and being assessed at a particular level of competence for that skill. However, learning packs can be created that discuss background knowledge for the skill, and what the student needs to know before performing the skill. There may also be health and safety or ethical issues to consider. Skills need practice; try giving students a chance to practise and get feedback so they are able to improve before being assessed. Once again, consider the assessment criteria and competency level for the skill.

Work-based learning

As the title suggests, learning here takes place in the workplace and can comprise short-term introductory experiences, paid work experience and a more formal training arrangement. The formal training agreement is an arrangement between the student, the employer and the educational institution, where tasks and criteria for monitoring and assessing the student are laid down.

In open learning

This very much depends on where the students will work. It may be that the workplace provides learning packs for them. However, if there is an arrangement between an educational institution and the employer, ensure all agree to the learning 'contract' set up and that the students are aware of any assessment as a result of it.

📖 **Work-based Learning Project**

University of Leeds

http://education.leeds.ac.uk/~edu/wblp/wblp.htm

This is an example of an approach taken by the University of Leeds.

Work Based Learning Modules in Degree Programmes at the University of Plymouth

http://sh.plym.ac.uk/eds/WBL_MODL.HTM

Tutorial-based learning

This is a standard didactic teaching method. The tutor prepares material to be learnt in a controlled, step-by-step manner with clear explanations and interactive exercises to encourage deep learning. Most computer-based learning packages use a tutorial style, some being more interactive than others. Textbooks are also pedagogically designed books with the novice in mind. Tutorials are quite time-consuming to write, so only select information that is not likely to change rapidly, for example stable facts, processes, procedures, rules and principles. Tutorial-based learning is excellent for the beginner and those wishing to get a basic grasp of essential principles. The more interactive the tutorial, the better it is for the learner.

In open learning

This is a standard format for open learning packs. Successful tutorials meet the needs of the students by being at the correct level, with concepts clearly explained and well laid out on the page. The more interactivity in the form of exercises, simulations and problem solving, the better. If this is truly open learning, make checks that the student is under-standing the work by asking for some of the exercises to be handed in. Offer 'clinic sessions' if there seems to be a problem.

Most of these approaches to independent learning are compliant with current thinking that learners don't fully understand information (deep learning) unless they have worked with the material intensively and reassembled it so that it has become part of their own experience – 'constructivist learning'. Jonassen (1992) refers to three stages of knowledge acquisition that could help with the instructional design of learning environments: the *introductory*, *advanced* and *expert* stages.

The *introductory* learning phase is reflected by well-structured domains with generally quite heavy guidance, which can be seen in activities such as drill and practice, question and answer, calculations and multiple-choice activities. This is very much the traditional instructional design and very evident in tutorials and computer-based learning packages. However, even at this early stage we must take care not to over-structure the material as it is important to leave 'room' for students to reflect and begin to work through ideas (however simple) themselves. Without reflection, it is very difficult for deep learning to take place (see Cross, 1995).

In Jonassen's *advanced* learning phase, intermediate learners will be able to deal with ill-structured domains (material that cannot be packaged into neat proven theories/concepts) where they start to solve complex problems and reassemble and extend information to make it fit a given context; this is a constructive phase. Some examples are problem solving and case-based activities. The variety of cases and problems will extend the learners' view of the subject domain, encouraging them to use information flexibly across situations in a similar way to experts.

Jonassen's third category, the *expert*, characteristically has a well-integrated cognitive structure of the subject, often drawing on information from adjacent knowledge domains as their expertise grows. It is this integration of information into a complex knowledge web that students are encouraged to develop. Therefore, moving from the structured learning environment to a research-led environment is one way that resource-based learning can lead students to a truly independent form of study. At this stage you will need to ensure that students' research skills are adequate.

For more approaches to instructional design, consult Reigeluth (1999). This is an excellent source where you can compare a wide variety of instructional design theories.

ACTIVITY 3C

A framework for self-directed learning

The framework below illustrates conditions characteristic of self-directed learning and was presented in a paper by Wilcox (1996). How do you think your teaching and your students' learning could be mapped to this framework?

Also consider:

- What is 'independent learning' for you or your department?
- What teaching and learning methods would you employ on a given course to encourage independent/self-directed learning? Consider the skills involved. Can you apply this to 'research-led teaching'?
- Are you conscious of varying these methods, or do you use your favourite, well-tried method most of the time?

Framework for self-directed learning

Structure

- flexible emergent plant, responsive to learner needs
- options for learner to make choices concerning:

participation	methods and materials
objectives	pace
content	evaluation

Climate	**Learner engagement**	**Learner competencies**
• supportive	• focus on problems of learners	• awareness of learning process
• collaborative	• learners are actively involved	• reflect on personal meaning
		• develop learning skills and strategies

Source: Susan Wilcox (1996)

Technology Enhanced Learning in Research Led Institutions (TELRI)

http://www.warwick.ac.uk/ETS/TELRI/

This is an HEFCE-funded TLTP3 project that seeks to develop ways of using technology-based materials and teaching methods to enhance students' capabilities as researchers. These are generally the broad capabilities of graduates that higher education has sought to develop, that employers value and that are of immense benefit in lifelong learning.

Linking Teaching and Research

Oxford Brookes University, UK

http://www.brookes.ac.uk/services/ocsd/link1/bib1/ltrbib.html

This is an excellent source.

3.2.2 A quick overview of writing open learning materials

In the pre-design phase:

- Be aware of the opportunities and constraints within your department (and within yourself) for developing this material – consider how educationally effective and efficient this method will be.
- Know your learner – are there any consistent misconceptions about your topic that should be addressed?
- Look at *all* the resources you have – include yourself, other tutors, peers, library, electronic resources, items in your room, etc.

In the design phase:

- Make the nature and structure of your pack clear: lead in learners, set learning outcomes, include 'maps' or overviews, advanced organizers (devices that help the student prepare for the learning to follow), case studies to illustrate application, and give summaries.
- Make your tutorial material as interactive as possible by:
  – presenting activities clearly;
  – avoiding trivial exercises, they only irritate;
  – varying activities, for example:
    – self-assessed questions,
    – multiple-choice questions,
    – true/false statements,
    – gap-filling exercises,
    – ordering tasks,
    – decision making using a case-based approach,

- being creative, applying reasoning, through problem solving,
- written assignments (such as essays, commentaries, summaries, flow charts, diagrams, reports, posters).

● Consider how the learner should respond to activities and how that work can be taken forward:
- With peers or alone?
- Will you include peer assessment? Have criteria for this been set up?
- Online quizzes with immediate mark and feedback?
- In their own log book, in the open learning pack, or on pages provided by the tutor?
- Will students be asked to hand in specific activities for a snapshot of how well they are doing? Will they know this in advance?
- Will key activities be assessed? Do they know which these are?
- What can they expect from tutor-assessed work?
- What about computer-marked tests? (See section 5.3.)

● Consider the layout of the material by adding visual material, leaving lots of white space, box texts for emphasis or asides. Too little white space on the page can make the material appear too dense.

● Supply other media that could be stored in a library as additional material. This should be very much 'additional' as students may have difficulty accessing it.

● Plan learner support, feedback and tutor marked assignments into the programme. Include good, timely feedback for students using activities to encourage reflective practice. Avoid the 'testing' approach unless really necessary.

Success Factors in Materials-based Learning

Derek Rowntree (1997)

http://www-iet.open.ac.uk/pp/D.G.F.Rowntree/MBL.htm/introdex.html

Neptuno: Open and Distance Learning Laboratory

http://fuev.adeit.uv.es/neptuno/english/

This was a two-year Socrates-funded project to improve the knowledge of open and distance learning products and methodologies. This laboratory is a comprehensive resource providing background information on building and developing Web-based materials to support learning and teaching. The resources range from pedagogical through to technical.

Explorations in Learning & Instruction: The theory into practice (TIP) database

http://www.gwu.edu/~tip/

TIP is a tool intended to make learning and instructional theory more accessible to educators. The database contains brief summaries of 50 major theories of learning and instruction. These theories can also be accessed according to learning domains and concepts.

📖   **Principles of Instructional Design: Web-based resources**

Richard Cain and Steve Purcell

http://dl.wju.edu/3472instrdesignres.htm

Discusses models of instructional design.

3.3   Planning resource bases for open learning environments

Resource-based learning is an holistic model of course design and encompasses a wide range of teaching and learning approaches. It can be seen as 'action learning' (Bourner and Flowers, 1997) integrating, for example, the opportunity to:

- disseminate information;
- develop students' capability to *use* ideas and information;
- develop students' ability to *generate* ideas and evidence;
- facilitate personal development;
- develop the capacity of students to *plan* and *manage* their own learning.

Resource-based learning is used in an open learning mode and can be defined as a wide range of multimedia teaching and learning materials crafted into a supportive learning environment. These environments comprise a variety of educational resources:

- *primary learning resources*, such as text, video, pictures, etc;
- *experiential learning resources,* such as problem solving, case studies, etc;
- *highly structured resources,* such as tutorials, computer aided learning, exercises and quizzes.

All these resources can reside within a resource base even though they offer quite different learning experiences; see Figure 3.2.

'Primary' resources emulate a library where students can search on key concepts according to their research query. The use of 'primary' here is meant to mean 'not structured pedagogically' – it is not literally a primary source in the true academic sense. These resources are ideal for areas of knowledge that are not easily reproduced in tutorial format, and provide an excellent environment for students to develop their research skills. It is here that the digital environment can be more efficient in that a large number of resources can be stored on a CD ROM or the Web with the added bonus of search facilities. However, you will need to reference original paper-based resources for this kind of learning as well as the many online journal databases, such as BIDS. For all primary sources, however, it is important that your students have good information handling (library) skills. The learning route (and scaffolding) here is determined by the questions posed by the student in relation to set work and reflects a research approach to learning.

📖 **A Report on Information Handling Skills and Resource Based Learning**

Janet McDonald and Robin Mason (1992)

http://www-iet.open.ac.uk/iet/otd/OTD101.html

📖 **BIDS Bibliographic Database**

http://www.bids.ac.uk

BIDS, run from Bath University and funded by JISC, was one of the first to provide widespread network access to commercially supplied bibliographic databases, free at the point of delivery. This service is available to anyone whose institution has registered, which applies to most universities in the UK. Users need to gain a username and password from their institution to have full use of the service. BIDS has also linked with Ingenta and together they provide 1000 full-text electronic journals. Restricted access is available through Ingenta for users who do not have a password.

Structured resources refer to pedagogically designed material with a highly focused learning route. The tutorial can ensure learning 'en-route' via self-assessment. This kind of learning material is good for information that can be well structured and for facts that don't change rapidly over time, eg processes and procedures. It is also ideal for the beginner. Once again, computer-based learning packages and World Wide Web tutorials have been developed for this learning approach. It is vital, however, that there are inter-active activities that encourage deep learning. The learning route here is determined by the tutorial itself, offering a very structured learning experience. Below is a selection of tutorials on the World Wide Web.

📖 **Netskills – Online Interactive Course (Tonic)**

http://www.netskills.ac.uk/

This online course/tutorial offers practical guidance on major Internet topics, ranging from basic through to advanced. The course as a whole is intended for beginners to networking, who have some familiarity with computers.

📖 **Engineering Materials**

http://www.soton.ac.uk/~pasr1/

The tutorial highlights include a pop-up glossary, an interactive phase diagram and formative quizzes.

Experience-based resources can comprise designed resources such as cases, problems, simulations and experiments as well as the students' personal experience they bring to the course. Hands-on resources encourage learning by 'doing' and can either precede overview material (ie, a bottom-up/inductive approach), or follow it (ie, a top-down/deductive approach). The learning route here is determined by the student in relation to the problem or cases set by the tutor. It provides an opportunity to integrate knowledge, be creative and work collaboratively.

The ability to incorporate both structured and less structured knowledge domains makes resource bases a very rich learning environment for a wide variety of learners. It also gives the system a longer shelf-life, and when students exhaust the structured environments, they can move to a more research style of learning where they can further develop their independent skills. To ensure good, focused use of the resource base, devise assignments and exercises, pose questions and set quizzes that allow students to interrogate the resources and reflect on their progress through direct feedback from the tutors, peers and/or computer-marked quizzes.

Janet McDonald and Robin Mason (1992) found that some students were overwhelmed by the quantity of information in resource-based learning courses. Ensure your students know *why* they are accessing the resources and have some criteria for them to assess when they have finished.

It is not necessary to incorporate all types of learning resource at once. You may wish to build up your resources incrementally. You could start with primary resources and some lecture notes and move on to tutorials and case-studies etc at a later date.

With this view of resource-based learning we are able to accommodate a variety of learning styles – from those quite happy with independence, to those needing more guidance and for those happier in the concrete empirical environment of 'hands on'.

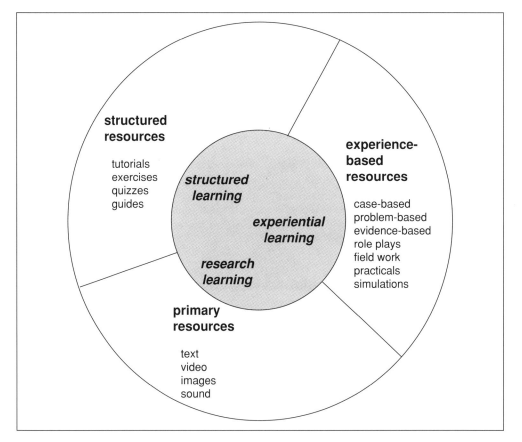

Figure 3.2 *Resources to encourage a multiple approach to learning*

ACTIVITY 3D

Searching for information on the Web

A

Using the World Wide Web search engine Lycos (http://www.lycos.com), find more information on David Kolb's model of experiential learning and consider how you could use this information in your teaching.

B

To speed up your searches, you can have several Web pages searching for you at the same time:

1. Right click on any link to the Lycos Web page.
2. Select 'Open link in new window' from the menu that appears.
3. A new window will appear and you can carry out a different search in that window.
4. Click between each window to access the information.

C

Try using some other search engines such as NorthernLight

http://www.northernlight.com/. This is quite good at finding academic sites. There is also Google at http://www.google.com/ with a very simple interface and no advertising. The most common academic search engine used at present is Altavista at http://www.altavista.com/. You need to try several search engines, as the results depend on the kind of search technique they use.

The Internet Detective

http://www.sosig.ac.uk/desire/internet-detective.html

This is a Web-based interactive tutorial (quizzes, teaching materials and exercises) looking at the skills needed to critically evaluate the quality of an Internet resource. It is aimed at both users and writers of Web pages.

3.3.1 Designing resource-based learning environments

In planning resource-based learning environments, we need to:

● Understand who the learners are.
● Understand the subject domain.
● Select pedagogically appropriate resources (primary, structured, experiential).
● Develop the technical skills to make these resources digital (see section 2.3).

- Develop educational expertise to bring all this together in a supportive learning environment (see section 3.2.1).
- Develop technical skills to implement the course – check the Active*Guide Web site with this book.

Assuming you are the content/domain specialist, you may need to seek assistance on the technical issues. It might be worth establishing who you can work with on the digitization of resources and the technical implementation of the course.

As we can see, when compiling resource-based learning we need to work at various levels (let's refer to these as 'models') simultaneously: the domain model, the learner model, the pedagogical model, the implementation model and the evaluation model. The resulting set of resources needs to result in a coherent learning environment for students. Table 3.2 gives a synopsis of the questions answered by each of the models.

Table 3.2

Learner Model	Pedagogical Model	Domain Model	Implementation Model	Evaluation Model
Answers the questions	Answers the questions	Answers the questions	Answers the questions	Answers the questions
■ *Who are the learners?* ■ *What do they know?* ■ *Do they have any critical misconceptions?* ■ *Are their technical skills adequate?*	■ *What are the values and philosophy of the course?* ■ *What are the learning outcomes?* ■ *How can the learning outcomes be realized?* ■ *How will they be assessed?*	■ *What do the students need to know at this level?* ■ *What is the curriculum?*	■ *What's the learning environment for the students?* ■ *How will they access resources?* ■ *How will they interact with each other and resources?*	■ *How well has this system worked in terms of pedagogy and efficiency?*

Learner model (who will be learning)

Determine:

- the needs of the students (academically and in terms of support needed during the course);
- how homogeneous/heterogeneous your learners are as a group;
- their IT skills;
- their expectations regarding an electronic resource base.

Domain model (what is to be learnt)

Determine:

- the level of the course to determine the type of content;
- what students need to know prior to the course (entry level);
- what students must *know* and *understand* at the end of the course (knowledge at exit); see also the pedagogical model;
- what students will be able to *do* at the end of the course (skills); see also the pedagogical model;
- a framework for cross-referencing/linking between resources to produce a coherent network of knowledge and learning materials;
- the resources needed: pictures, videos, diagrams, practical, lecture notes, tutorials, simulations, case studies, etc; see the implementation model.

Pedagogical model (how will they learn)

- Write a course description and learning outcomes – for content and skills.
- Consider the pedagogical values and philosophy for the course, eg if you are encouraging independent learning, collaborative learning, a reflective approach, etc, do the materials and your management of the course allow this to happen? The 'climate' you create should reflect the values.
- Select resources from the domain model to reflect a structured, a research and/or an experiential approach to learning – decide if you are starting with particular kinds of resources (eg, just primary resources or quizzes) or a mixture. The kind of resources you select will depend on your students and the domain. For example, beginners may feel more secure in a more structured environment. Start by planning the concept for the full resource base, as this will be helpful when you come to add more information later. It is advisable to develop it incrementally.
- Consider what your students will *do* with the resources – plan a focus for learning and develop scaffolding techniques – this is your pedagogical model. Decide what students will do with the different kinds of resources and how they can be integrated. Will this activity comply with the learning outcomes? Which interactive activities can you use: quizzes, exercises, question-answer, FAQs (frequently asked questions)?
- Consider the mechanism for managing this resource as well as student feedback and communication to complete the learning cycle (tutor marked assignments, peer review, computer marked quizzes).
- Determine the mode of assessment to reflect the knowledge and skills learnt on the course.

The Web: Design for Active Learning

Katy Campbell (1999) Technologies for Learning, University of Alberta, Canada

http://www.atl.ualberta.ca/articles/idesign/activel.cfm

An excellent site offering ideas on course interactivity and instructional design.

Implementation model (how the material will be delivered)

- Select appropriate technology to *create* your resources (see section 2.3 and the Active*Guide).

- Select appropriate technology to *deliver* your resources:

  – as individual resources via the network or housed on a Web site and delivered via the Internet;

  – as a compilation of resources in a learning environment delivered via a CD ROM or the Web (see section 3.3.2);

  – as a paper-based set of resources with additional multimedia elements;

  – check your resources allow for universal accessibility and, if you have students who are unable to access your resources, whether you can find ways of adjusting your resources to allow for access (see section 2.2.4);

  – check where you can either learn how to do these things yourself or where you can get help;

  – check the local procedures at your institution for delivering resources to students.

The evaluation model (how successful was it – what improvements can be made?)

- Evaluate for educational quality

  – look at the academic content, range and depth of material, pedagogical effectiveness of resources chosen, achievement of learning outcomes and management of the course.

- Evaluate for usability of the learning environment

  – look at students' understanding of the course and what they thought was expected of them, their ability to handle the environment (IT skills, finding and using material, layout of the environment), gaining access to the resources.

- Evaluate for efficiency (cost-effectiveness)

  – give reasons why this method was chosen (number of students, type of material, widening access, key skills, etc), estimate the amount of time spent implementing this resource, estimate the amount of time you will need to keep it running in subsequent years, the shelf-life of the course, establish the learning hours/student over the course (with open learning material it is important to estimate learning hours, indicating how many of them are in face-to-face teaching sessions).

If you are interested in pursuing this in greater depth, there are plenty of Web resources that can give you detailed information on how to do this. It is preferable for you to pursue your own research here as it is a very wide area. Below are some resources to get you started. For another view of a model to integrate learning technologies, see Stoner (1997), and for a framework for evaluating educational technology, see Oliver (1998).

Evaluation Cookbook

A Learning Technology Dissemination Initiative – LTDI

http://lomond.icbl.hw.ac.uk/ltdi/cookbook

An excellent resource for all aspects of evaluation. It can be viewed online or downloaded on to your desktop where you can then print it out.

Criteria for Selecting Educational Delivery Methods: Samples from the literature

Carolyn Kotlas, Center for Instructional Technology, University of North Carolina

http://www.unc.edu/cit/guides/irg-13.html

ACTIVITY 3E

Conduct a review of C&IT in learning and teaching to show an understanding of the underlying educational processes

You could:

- Evaluate a range of learning technologies and identify their strengths and weaknesses.
- Produce a flow diagram of the decision making process you took in selecting the technology.
- Assess the effectiveness of selected technology in relation to the educational processes such as independent learning, reflective practice, student scholarship and equal opportunities.

(Taken from the EFFECTS programme – see the appendix at the end of this chapter for the seven generic learning outcomes used on the programme, and section 1.3.2 for information about the EFFECTS programme.)

3.3.2 Creating a resource-based learning Web site

Hypermedia entails linking (cross-referencing) text, images, video and audio files, while hypertext is the linking of text only. We are now quite familiar with this kind of browsing when using the Web or CD ROMS where coloured text highlights the links. The ease of making these links, giving us instant access to resources around the world, and the increasing ease of making multimedia resources, have been major factors in popularizing hypermedia and in particular the Web. This technological revolution has fuelled the notions of the virtual university and global education and we are seeing the development of e-education along with e-commerce, e-business, e-lib(rary), e-mail and e-banking (see section 1.1). Therefore, education and hypermedia are now inextricably bound together.

Having course information on the Web can mean many different things to different people, ranging from a purely administrative function to a full learning environment; see Table 3.3.

Generally speaking, there are plenty of Web sites reflecting options 1 and 2, and far fewer reflecting option 3. The first two options are not embedding the Web in teaching, and they tend to be 'bolt on' Web sites with ad hoc resources appearing as the lecturer has time and know-how to upload them. Option 3, on the other hand, does reflect a qualitative shift in the use of the Web and an embedding of the technology. This equally applies to learning environments delivered via CD ROM.

Table 3.3

Web site type	Contains	Purpose
Course administrative site – often produced at a departmental level **1**	■ List of courses, seminars and tutorials ■ Departmental 'rules' ■ Opening/closing times ■ Exam timetable ■ Staff contact details (possibly) ■ The information is constantly available to all	■ Often used for marketing to potential students ■ Supports the administrative staff in not having to continually give out the same information ■ Cuts down on photocopies
Individual lecturers' pages – produced at an individual lecturer level **2**	■ Lists of publications ■ Areas of research interest ■ Sometimes areas of other interest ■ Courses taught ■ Can house resources for individual courses ■ Students get to know about their lecturer	■ Gives the lecturer a profile within and beyond the university ■ Acts as a 'filing cabinet' for student resources ■ Becomes a public archive of what that lecturer does
A learning environment – often produced at an individual level **3**	■ Course overview ■ Course ground rules ■ List of participants and tutors ■ Course units ■ Resources ■ Assignments ■ Exam information ■ Communications area	■ Provides a wide range of information concerning the course ■ Assignments to give focus to the learning ■ Resources for study ■ Communications for collaborative learning

Structuring a learning environment

When we structure a learning environment we need to consider both the macro structure and the cognitive structure. The macro structure gives the learner an overview of the scope of the resources, and how the material is organized. The cognitive structure is a reflection of how the resources are semantically linked to give a coherent set of resources.

The macro structure

Your first consideration is in creating a *home page* that will act as the 'front door' and give your course an identity. There will be several other pages that offer a macro structure for the course that will allow students to navigate the environment easily. Figure 3.3 is an example of a simple home page for a course.

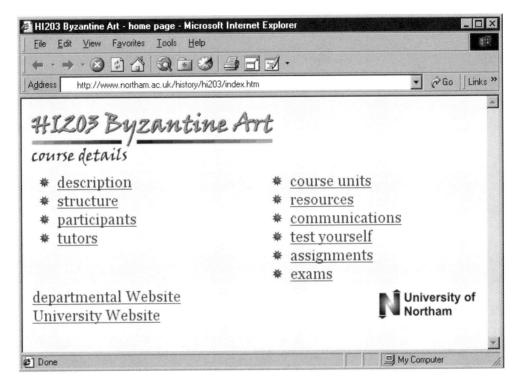

Figure 3.3   *A sample home page for course resources*

If we follow the links on *description, course structure, participants* and *tutors,* we may find the items shown in Table 3.4.

If we follow the links on *course units,* it could be organized according to teaching scenarios such as 'lectures', 'seminars' etc, or under topic. At this level you need to also cover the aims of the unit and the learning outcomes. Make sure the aims and learning outcomes for your unit tie in with the overall course aims and outcomes. You will also be considering the different types of learning and teaching scenarios. An example for 'Topic 1' linked according to teaching scenarios is shown in Table 3.5, and linked according to topic in Table 3.6.

Table 3.4

Description	Structure	Participants	Tutors
■ Aims ■ Learning outcomes	■ How structured – lectures/seminars/ tutorials/practicals ■ Topic titles ■ What's expected of students: course ground rules, expected approach to learning eg independent learning, assignments	■ A list of who's on the course with e-mail addresses	■ A list of tutors and possibly post-graduate teaching assistants with e-mail addresses
Answers the question: What's this course about and what should I know at the end of it?	*Answers the question: How's the course organized?*	*Answers the question: Who else is on the course and how can I contact them?*	*Answers the question: How can I get help when I need it?*

Table 3.5

Lectures	Seminars	Tutorials	Practical/Field/ Clinical Work
■ Aims ■ Learning Outcomes ■ Topics ■ Resources: tutor provided, external links, reading list	■ Aims ■ Learning Outcomes ■ Topics ■ What students have to do (possibly refer to 'questions' under 'activities' below)	■ Aims ■ Learning Outcomes ■ Topics ■ What students have to do (possibly to 'exercises' under 'activities' below)	■ Aims ■ Learning Outcomes ■ Topics ■ Resources: tutor provided, external links, reading list ■ Details for practical work (report writing templates, ground rules, etc)
Activities: quizzes, questions and exercises (applicable across all scenarios) Across the teaching scenarios, make sure that students see how the topics link up and have complementary learning outcomes			

The structure up to this point has been very hierarchical and gives you a global macro structure within which to place resources. This should make it easier for your students to navigate.

Table 3.6

Topic A	Assignments	Resources	Teaching	Group Work
■ Title of topic with some description ■ Aims ■ Learning outcomes	■ List of assignments – not all to be assessed. You may want to allow students to decide which assignments out of a particular type they hand in are for assessment ■ Note criteria for assessment especially in collaborative projects	■ All the resources you have gathered ■ State if they are primary resources (could refer to this as the 'library') or structured resources (refer to as 'learning materials')	■ List face-to-face sessions and location	■ Indicate your view on collaborative work ■ List of assignments ■ Allocate groups

The cognitive (coherent) structure: linking your resources

When you start linking your resources you need to decide the kind of linking structure you want and how you can apply it to both primary and learning resources.

Primary resources can be linked together in several ways, depending on the nature of the subject matter and how necessary it is to read each node (a chunk of information) linearly. If this is vital, then a hierarchical structure is better. You can restrict movement between nodes by only allowing cross-linking at particular points. In Figure 3.4 ('Hierarchy') we can see that the reader always has to move up to the previous level in order to access to the next node. So, to read information at node A.1.3.2, level 4, the learner can only reach that piece of information by moving from A1 through A.1.3 to A.1.3.2. Even if the reader is already at level 4, he or she cannot just move to the neighbouring node. This gives the author/tutor maximum control over how the resources are accessed, but can be rather tedious for the learner, unless it is really necessary.

With the network model it is the opposite. Here almost everything is linked to everything else. This is a so-called semantic net. It is quite easy for the author to get carried away here and link things that are only mildly connected – try to avoid this. If you are using a network, then decide on a link strategy. Are you linking across authors, concepts, lines of argumentation, etc? Are your learners aware of this strategy?

The mixed model is exactly what it means. You can use hierarchical linking to a particular level in the structure and then link on a network basis. This gives some navigational support for the learner, but also the freedom to work within a semantic network, allowing the learner to move between all nodes at a given level. In Figure 3.4 ('Mixed') levels 1 and 2 are hierarchical and level 3 is a network of inter-linked nodes.

Learning materials such as exercises, on the other hand, could have a structure as illustrated in Figure 3.5.

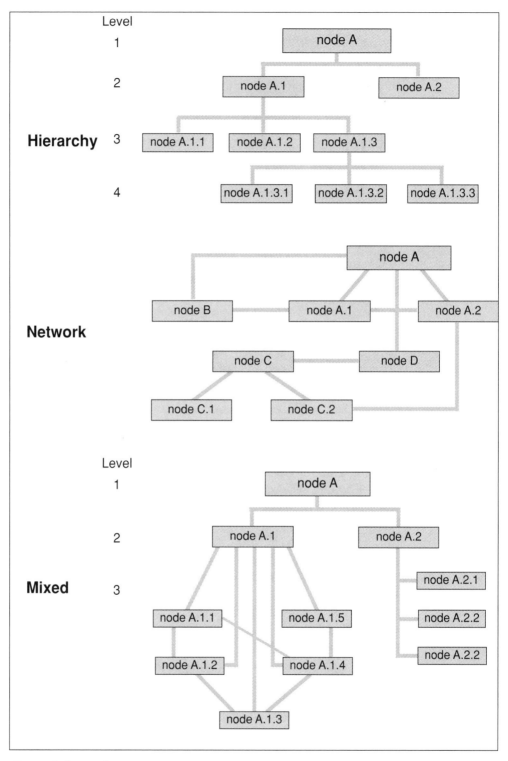

Figure 3.4 *Linking resources*

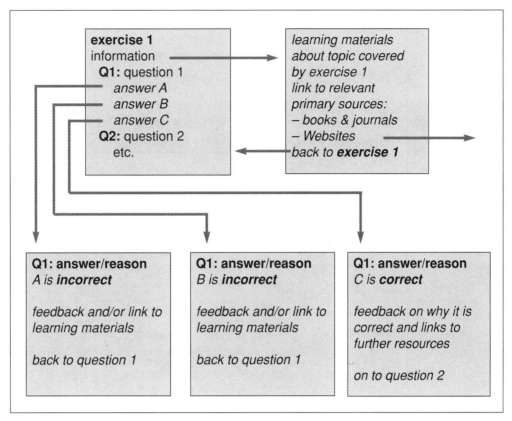

Figure 3.5   *Developing learning routines*

This framework for learning routines emphasizes the *learning* of the routines rather than 'right' or 'wrong' aspects. If you require a more assessment-style approach where the results can be recorded, see section 5.3.

Learning materials involving case studies may be structured as in Figure 3.6. This example is taken from a medical/social work perspective, but of course can be adapted.

For the student, 'your task' here could be:

● Read the notes of the case study, diagnose the problem and establish a programme for clinical management. Write a report on the case for another professional who may be involved. Provide a proforma for the appropriate style of document that should be written.

● An alternative could be that students write smaller reports from different professional perspectives. This gives them insight into multiple perspectives of a given case and encourages 'cognitive flexibility' – overcoming the tendency to address problems from one perspective.

The overall structure of this may be as shown in Figure 3.7.

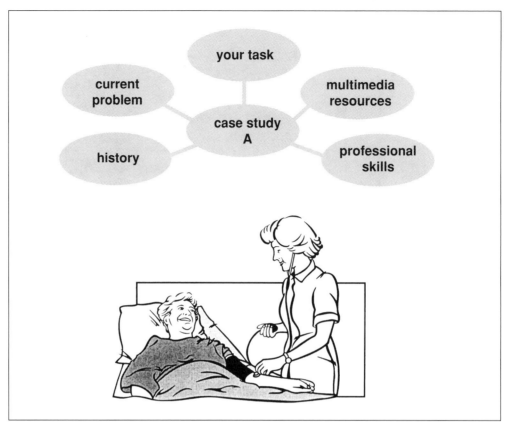

Figure 3.6 *Building up a case study*

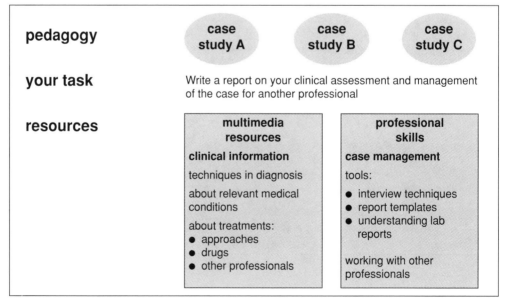

Figure 3.7 *Pedagogical resources for a case study*

ACTIVITY 3F

Determine learning outcomes

Look at the structure of the case study example above (Figure 3.7) and determine (as far as possible) the learning outcomes for the student in terms of *cognitive* and *professional skills*. For more information on writing learning objectives see section 5.2.1.

 ### Principles of Instructional Design: Web-based resources

Richard Cain and Steve Purcell

http://dl.wju.edu/e472instrdesignres.htm

Discusses models of instructional design.

 ### Resource-based Learning

http://web.wwa.com/~cfox/alice/rbl.htm

A series of three articles by Carol Fox.

ACTIVITY 3G

Design and plan a strategy for integrating appropriate technology in your teaching

Consider a course you are offering that you think could be suitable for resource-based learning and benefit from redesigning. You could:

- Provide a rationale for restructuring an existing course/unit/session and say why you wish to make changes.
- Provide a rationale (course/unit specification) for your restructured course/unit/session.
- Specify the learning outcomes for the restructured course/unit.
- Indicate how your use of C&IT supports the learning outcomes of your restructured course/unit/session.
- Specify how your teaching style or methods will change as a result of this restructuring.

(Taken from the EFFECTS programme – see the appendix at the end of this chapter for the seven generic learning outcomes used on the programme, and section 1.3.2 for information about the EFFECTS programme.)

✍ **ACTIVITY 3H**

Checklist: when using digital learning resources (for Chapters 2 and 3)

1. Are the text documents you need word-processed?	Yes ☐ No ☐	If 'yes', do you know how to insert hyperlinks in your document and convert it into an html documents for the Web? If you don't, check out the Active*Guide for some help. If 'no', this is something you should do as a priority. Check with your institution how you can learn word-processing and get access to the software.
2. Will you need photographs or slides?	Yes ☐ No ☐	If 'yes', how will you process them – a photo CD or scanned images? Do you have the software to view photos from the CD or the hardware to scan images? Do you have anyone to help you? What is the educational value of using these images – are they worth the effort? See Active*Guide.
3. Are your lecture notes in a presentation system like Microsoft PowerPoint?	Yes ☐ No ☐	If 'no', you may want to learn how to do this. Check out section 2.3 and the Active*Guide to help you get started. Once you have your notes in a presentation system, you can then make them available over your local network or put them on the Web for delivery. *Note:* if you use the Web, don't forget to include additional information, activities, and links to make this a real resource for your students.
4. Will you need sound?	Yes ☐ No ☐	If 'yes', do you know how to digitize, or have access to someone who could do it for you? What are the pedagogical reasons for using the sound – will it really add to your set of resources? Check out the Active*Guide.

5.

| Will you need graphics, video or animations? | Yes ☐ No ☐ | If 'yes', consider getting help with these resources until you are comfortable with the technology. These can be time-consuming. Make sure the educational value of using them outweighs the time you (and others) need to invest in producing them. Check out the Active*Guide. |

6.

| Do you have a grasp on how you can fit all your resources together into a coherent learning environment? | Yes ☐ Not sure ☐ | If 'not sure', check out section 3.3. |

7.

I understand that:

| a) Resource-based learning (RBL) is a form of open learning and that students will need skills in independent learning to be successful | Yes ☐ Not sure ☐ | If 'not sure', check out section 1.2, section 2.1 and 3.2.1. |

| b) RBL encompasses a wide range of resources (primary, pedagogical, experiential) and the educational implications of each of these resources | Yes ☐ Not sure ☐ | If 'not sure', check out section 3.3. |

| c) Creating RBL in a hypermedia environment entails various approaches to structuring the information | Yes ☐ Not sure ☐ | If 'not sure', check out section 3.3.1. |

| d) Assessment may be different for students working within a RBL environment, however, it needs to be compliant with the set of learning outcomes | Yes ☐ Not sure ☐ | If 'not sure', check out Chapter 5. |

| e) You may be expected to evaluate your approach, even though you may not have to do this with traditional teaching methods | Yes ☐ Not sure ☐ | If 'not sure', check out section 3.3.1. |

8.

Are your students 'well equipped' to work in an electronic environment?	Yes ☐ Not ☐ sure	This is a very broad question and you should consider at least the following:

- the number of computers available to your students (as well as the accessibility of them). See section 2.2.
- the need to train your students in using your software. Will they need any other technical support?
- Do your students really know what to do with the resources?
- Is the purpose of the tasks and the learning outcomes clear to students?
- Check your pedagogical approach.
- Are your resources universally accessible to disadvantaged students?

9.

If you create a Web resource-based learning environment, you understand:

a) the kind of web site you want to develop and why	Yes ☐ Not ☐ sure	If you are 'not sure', check why you are thinking of using the Web, why this particular course and the benefits you envisage (in quality and efficiency terms).
b) that you will include a wide range of resources i.e. primary, pedagogical and experiential	Yes ☐ Not ☐ sure	If you are 'not sure' about this and find it daunting, start with some aspect of the course and then build upon it. Do try and have a plan on how the site will develop.
c) that you have to develop a strategy for linking your primary resources	Yes ☐ Not ☐ sure	It is important to know how you are linking your resources – there are no set ways, but devise a system and try to keep to it: are you following through lines of argument, links to other authors, contrary views?
d) how to produce suitable pedagogical material for open learning ie: tutorials, quizzes, case studies, problem solving and other exercise types that promote learning	Yes ☐ Not ☐ sure	If you are 'not sure' about this, check out the Active*Guide for some help and see section 3.3.
e) that the learning outcomes and student tasks should be made clear within the resources	Yes of course ☐	I think we all agree with this, we just have to make it really explicit, especially in open learning where it is so easy to overlook these points.

10.			
Are you aware of the procedures for putting resources on to your institution's network or Web server?	Yes ☐ No ☐	If 'no', check this out early on. Sometimes there is a long delay before you can upload software on to the network due to working practices of your institution. Other organizations may insist that your web site has a certain look that is compliant with the organizational culture. Does your institute have an accessibility policy with regard to web sites? It is worth clearing all of these issues before you start.

Appendix

The Learning Outcomes for the EFFECTS Programme

This programme examines the application and integration of C&IT in learning environments, together with the opportunities and constraints this imposes. You will need to reflect on the process as well as report the outcome of your action research.

You will need to demonstrate that you have achieved the seven learning outcomes for the programme. This will be achieved via your portfolio, which will mainly comprise a report of your case study. You will need to develop a strategy for support and training (where relevant).

Outcome 1: Conducted a review of C&IT in learning and teaching and shown an understanding of the underlying educational processes

This will include evidence that you have: *conducted a review of appropriate learning technologies and their applications and reasons for selecting a particular C&IT solution in your case study.*

You might evidence this outcome by:

- Evaluating a range of learning technologies and identifying their strengths and weaknesses in relation to your case study.
- Producing a flow diagram of the decision making process you took in selecting the technology you chose so that someone else could benefit from your experience.
- Assessing the effectiveness of selected technology in relation to the educational processes such as: independent learning, reflective practice, student scholarship and equal opportunities.

Outcome 2: Analysed opportunities and constraints in using C&IT and selected C&IT appropriate to the learning situation (of your case study)

This will include evidence that you have: *carried out an IT audit to identify resource availability and constraints within your institution (department), analysed the learning needs of students regarding the use of selected C&IT.*

You might evidence this outcome by:

- Conducting an audit of the practicalities of using your selected technology within your institution.
- Indicating (when appropriate) why your chosen technology (on educational grounds – see outcome 1) could not be used and identifying the next best technological solution.
- Conducting an audit of the needs of your students (and other members of staff involved with this course/unit) in relation to their using this technology.

Outcome 3: Designed and planned a strategy for integrating appropriate C&IT

This will include evidence that you have: *designed and planned a strategy for (re)structuring a course/unit according to pedagogic principles and the integration of appropriate C&IT. The strategy should include an evaluation plan (see outcome 5).*

You might evidence this outcome by:

- Providing a rationale for restructuring an existing course/unit and why you wish to make changes.
- Providing a rationale (course/unit specification) for your restructured course/unit.
- Specifying the learning outcomes for the restructured course/unit.
- Indicating how your use of C&IT supports the learning outcomes of your restructured course/unit.
- Specifying how your teaching style or methods will change as a result of this restructuring.
- Specifying how the learning outcomes will be assessed. If this is not appropriate to your particular case study, indicate how you could assess these learning outcomes.
- Providing a timed plan for implementing your new course/unit re pedagogical redesign, selecting and learning new technology, readapting pedagogical materials, etc.
- Determining how you will evaluate your innovation (see outcome 5).
- Documenting your reflections of this process.

Outcome 4: Implemented a developed strategy

This will include evidence that you have: *demonstrated basic project management and/or teamwork skills in implementing your strategy. Piloted a course using technology-supported learning. Enabled students to use the learning technologies effectively and supported the learning process as appropriate (eg, for academic staff, delivered the course and assessed students).*

You might evidence this outcome by:

- Indicating how you initiated various 'teams' in support of your innovation (eg, with fellow academic staff and academic support units).

- Developing a new teaching style in light of the restructured approach and conveying this to your students (ie, explicitly identifying course philosophy, learning outcomes, tutor/student roles on the course/unit).

- Developing support strategies for students in terms of their using the new technology.

- Collecting data in support of your evaluation (see outcome 5).

- Documenting your reflections of this process.

- Assessing students' learning outcomes where appropriate.

Outcome 5: Evaluated impact of the interventions

This will include evidence that you have: *evaluated the impact of the incorporation of technology on students and colleagues. Maintained an awareness of external changes and made adaptations as necessary.*

You might evidence this outcome by:

- Selecting and implementing a suitable evaluation method for your case study.

- Reporting on your findings within your case study 'report', including an estimation of the time and cost involved in the innovation and any gains you have observed in terms of the efficiency and effectiveness of the new structure.

- Indicating in your case study report modifications you would make as a result of your evaluation findings and any implications that may arise as a result.

- Documenting your reflections and those of your colleagues regarding the whole process.

Outcome 6: Disseminated the findings of the evaluation

This will include evidence that you have: *provided feedback for students and colleagues and disseminated experience and findings to the department or more widely.*

You might evidence this outcome by:

- Writing a case study report of your action research/innovation. Consider writing this document for publication.

- Giving a workshop/presentation to your colleagues on your experience and the outcomes of the project.

- Giving feedback to students on the outcomes of the project.

- Writing a reflective document on the process of this project.

Outcome 7: Reviewed, planned and undertook appropriate actions related to your own CPD (continuing professional development)

This will include evidence that you have: *reviewed your needs in relation to embedding*

C&IT and made an appropriate CPD action plan to meet your individual requirements. Undertaken your own CPD and shown how you have incorporated this into your implementation plan.

You might evidence this outcome by:

- Conducting a needs analysis of your own professional development needs.
- Prioritizing your needs and finding ways of supporting them (eg, where to obtain CPD, the cost, your time in relation to the department's needs, in relation to your case study).
- Recording any CPD activities you attend, mailbases and other discussion groups or networks you belong to.
- Recording meetings with your mentor.

References

Boud, D and Feletti, G (1992) *The Challenge of Problem Based Learning*, Kogan Page, London

Bourner, T and Flowers, S (1997) 'Teaching and learning methods in higher education: a glimpse of the future', *Reflections on Higher Education*, **9**, pp 77–10

Bruce, C (1998) 'The phenomenon of information literacy', *Higher Education Research & Development,* **17** (1)

Cross, P (1995) 'Teaching and learning in the next century', http://www.ntlf.com/html/sf/teaching.htm

DeRoure, D, Carr, L, Hall, W and Hill, G (1995) 'Enhancing web support for resource based learning', http://www.mmrg.ecs.soton.ac.uk/publications/papers/conference95/workshop.html

Gibbs, B (1989) 'Designing learning packages', Module 8 in *Certificate in Teaching in Higher Education by Open Learning*, Oxford Centre for Staff Development

Gunn, C (1999) 'They love it, but do they learn from it? Evaluating the educational impact of innovations', *Higher Education Research & Development*, **18** (2), pp 185–99

Hannafin, M, Land, S and Oliver, K (1999) 'Open learning environments: foundations, methods and models', in ed C M Reigeluth, *Instructional-design Theories and Models, Volume II: A new paradigm of instructional theory*, Lawrence Erlbaum, London

Jonassen, D (1992) 'Evaluating constructivist learning', in eds T Duffy and D Jonassen, *Constructivism and the Technology of Instruction: A conversation*, Lawrence Erlbaum, London, pp 137–48

Laverty, C (1997) 'Resource-based learning', http://stauffer.queensu.ca/inforef/tutorials/rbl/index.htm

Lockyer, L, Patterson, J and Harper, B (1999) 'Measuring effectiveness of health education in a web-based learning environment: a preliminary report', *Higher Education Research & Development*, **18** (2), pp 233–46

McConnell, D (1995) *Implementing Computer-supported Cooperative Learning*, Kogan Page, London

McDonald, J and Mason, R (1992) 'Handling information skills and resource based learning', http://www-iet.open.ac.uk/iet/otd/OTD101.html

Naylor, M (1997) 'Work-based learning', *Eric Digest*, 187, http://ericacve.org/docs/dig187.htm

Oliver, M (1998) 'A framework for evaluating the use of educational technology', http://legacy.unl.ac.uk/latid/elt/report1.htm

Pollard, N (1996) 'Issues raised by implementing RBL within higher education institutions', published by DeLiberations, http://www.lgu.ac.uk/deliberations/rbl/pollard.html

Race, P (1992) *53 Interesting Ways to Write Open Learning Materials*, Technical and Educational Services, Bristol

Reeves, T and Laffey, J (1999) 'Design, assessment and evaluation of a problem-based learning environment in undergraduate engineering', *Higher Education Research & Development*, **18** (2), pp 219–32

Reigeluth, C M (ed) (1999) *Instructional-Design Theories and Models, Volume II: A new paradigm of instructional theory*, Lawrence Erlbaum, London

Riesbeck, C K, and Schank, R S (1989) *Inside Case-based Reasoning*, Lawrence Erlbaum, Northvale, NJ

Robertson, S (1996) 'A pragmatic look at some of the issues faced by those who seek to produce and deliver resource based learning (RBL) in higher education', published by DeLiberations, http://www.lgu.ac.uk/deliberations/rbl/robertson.html

Sackett, D L, Rosenberg, W M C, Gray, J A M, Haynes, R B and Richardson, W S (1996) 'Evidence-based medicine: what it is and what it isn't', http://cebm.jr2.ox.ac.uk/ebmisisnt.html#coredef. (This article is based on an editorial from the *British Medical Journal*, 1996, 312, 71–2)

Stoner, G (1997) 'A conceptual framework for the integration of learning technology', http://www.icbl.hw.ac.uk/ltdi/implementing-it/frame.htm

Waugh, R (1998) 'The course experience questionnaire: a Rasch measurement model of analysis', *Higher Education Research and Development*, **17** (1), pp 45–64

Wilcox, S (1996) 'Fostering self-directed learning in the university setting', *Studies in Higher Education*, **21** (2), pp 165–76

4 Using communication technologies to facilitate learning

Although the Web is an excellent medium for accessing information and tutorial materials, it is the use of the Internet for communication that arguably promises the greatest educational benefits for higher education. If planned and managed well, communication technologies can be used to facilitate the development of online communities in which all participants collaborate to discuss, reflect on and deepen their understanding of their learning.

In this chapter we will discuss:

- the nature of learning, teaching and working together in online groups (4.1);
- techniques for structuring online discussions (4.2);
- guidelines for effective facilitation of online discussions (4.3);
- other ways in which electronic communications can be used (4.4);
- the technologies available to support communication (4.5).

4.1 Online discussion in groups

We know that seminars are most effective when they are regular and frequent, so that the discussions are relevant to current course topics. However, rising student numbers, modularized courses and part-time learners make it increasingly difficult for us to schedule and run small-group discussion seminars face-to-face. Proponents of 'online seminars' argue that they can not only overcome these problems but also help us facilitate higher-quality debate than that typically present in face-to-face seminars.

The key advantages ascribed to online seminars are:

- You and your students can participate at any convenient time and place – all that is needed is a PC with Internet access. In addition, the seminar will usually be available seven days a week as a forum for debate throughout the duration of the course, rather than at infrequent fixed times.
- Contributions are typed, not spoken. This gives everyone time to prepare their arguments carefully and include any quotes or references needed. It equalizes the opportunities to contribute, so that students who prefer to think before they speak,

or speak English as a second language, are not disadvantaged. It also minimizes bias due to gender, race or disability issues – people are valued because of their contributions to the debate.

● The discussions are recorded as a series of messages that can be viewed and reviewed, summarized, quoted and archived. Selected messages can be reused by you to spur debate in subsequent seminars, or as the basis for a 'frequently asked questions' list to assist future classes.

There are also some disadvantages to be aware of:

● Everyone needs frequent and convenient access to suitable PCs. For students the best solution is their own PC with Internet access. All participants need computing skills, including typing, and access to adequate technical support.

● You need to carefully prepare and moderate the discussions so that they are inclusive, centred and critical. Too few messages each week and the seminar will wither; too many and students will be overwhelmed. How much time should the students be expected to spend on this activity each week? How much of your time is required for effective moderation?

● Students do not get to practise verbal communication skills and having to 'think on their feet'. It is therefore a good idea to retain some face-to-face seminars.

ACTIVITY 4A

Thinking about discussion and communication in your courses

You should use the activities in this chapter to guide you through the process of embedding online communications within an existing course – so you will need to pick a suitable course from those you teach and use it as the basis of each activity. You could also use them to plan how online communications might be used in a new course, provided you interpret the questions in that context.

How much use do you make of discussion or collaborative work in this course?

☐ central to course   ☐ a good deal   ☐ not much   ☐ none

If 'none' or 'not much', could using electronic communications help you manage the learning (section 4.4.1)? Alternatively, you might want to think about changing the way you teach the course to make greater use of discussion or collaboration between students.

Do you encourage discussion during lectures or is it confined to seminars and tutorials?

☐ lectures include discussion   ☐ seminars   ☐ tutorials   ☐ other sessions

Looking at your answers, when do your students get the opportunity to discuss the course with you and each other?

How many time-tabled hours of small-group work are there on the course? _____

(a) How many hours in total is this for you and any teaching assistants?_____

(b) How many hours does each student spend? _____

Is that a good ratio of staff to student time? (divide answer b by answer a).

List any recent situations in which it would have been very useful to easily and quickly send a message, reference or resource to all the students on the course.

4.1.1   The experience of learning in online groups

As tutors, when we think about starting to use online communications to facilitate learning, one of the difficulties we often face is that we have no experience of participation. We can remember what it was like to be a student in a lecture, seminar or tutorial, but have never learnt as part of an online group. In these groups, tutors and students share and discuss information, experience and knowledge by exchanging text messages that all members of the group can read. Some institutions provide appropriate professional development by enrolling tutors in online courses that not only teach the necessary skills and knowledge, but also provide a taste of what it is like to be a student learning online. This chapter recognizes that many of us will not have the opportunity to participate in such courses, and attempts to provide guidance that will help us learn 'on the job' as we set up and run our first online groups.

The following fictional account hopefully gives a flavour of what participation is like for a student:

> Jenna is a part-time student studying Social Science at the University of Northam. Two days a week she travels 20 miles to attend lectures at the campus but the rest of the course is conducted online in the Virtual Tutorial (or VeeTee as it is usually called). She usually participates in this three or four times a week, but it really depends on how tired she is when she gets home from work or how busy her weekend is. She uses her home PC, modem and Internet connection to access the VeeTee – the phone bill is often £10 a week, but that is still much less than her travel costs to the campus.
>
> Once she has used her username and password to access the VeeTee, she reads all the new messages that have been posted since her last visit. With 30 people in her class, there are often 50 or more messages to look at, but many are short and only take a few seconds to read. Some of the others are from her project group, and she copies-and-pastes these to her word-processor for later review. There is also an ongoing discussion about recent government legislation that she has been contributing to, and she posts replies to a couple of messages about this.

She then disconnects to save her phone bill while she re-reads the project messages. She is working with four other students to analyse data obtained from online census databases and present their findings as a Web site so that the rest of the class can comment. She does an hour's work on the project, including typing responses to her co-workers' queries and suggestions.

Finally, she reconnects to the VeeTee and copies-and-pastes her responses into new messages to her project group. Another 10 messages have been posted during the evening – and one of them is from a tutor to say that he is ill and won't be giving his lecture the following morning. That means Jenna can take a later (and cheaper) train to the campus and use the morning to catch up on some reading.

So where does the learning take place? Some of it happens online, when she reads a wide range of views, some from her tutors but most from her peers, about a topic such as recent government legislation. A lot of it happens offline, when she thinks about these views, conducts relevant research and formulates her responses. There is also vicarious learning, in which she follows but does not contribute to discussions on other topics – she is happy just to observe since there is a limit to the time available for her active participation. She is also able to review discussion topics, to see how they started and developed and maybe reflect on how her understanding has changed because of those discussions.

It may also be worth imagining what it would be like to be the tutor on such a course:

Henry is the tutor managing the Virtual Tutorial group for second-year Social Science students studying part-time at the University of Northam. It suits his face-to-face teaching commitment to log in on Tuesdays, Wednesdays and Fridays, although he sometimes fits in short additional sessions if things are busy or particularly interesting. Although he allows two hours for each session, they often take less – at least once the course is well underway and the students are used to the system.

His usual routine is to check for any personal messages sent to him by the students and deal with those first, then quickly browse the discussion forums looking at the message subject lines. This gives him an idea of how busy the forums are and which topics are attracting the most interest. He skim-reads all the messages and decides if any of them need his input before going back and typing a few responses. Finally, he uses the software to see when the students last accessed the system and notes that three of them haven't logged on since last week – not critical, but something to keep an eye on.

Sometimes the discussions will show that the students have not grasped some point, in which case he makes a note to look again at how that part of the course is taught. At other times, he copies a query and its answer from the forum to a Web page of 'frequently asked questions' that students can always refer to. These are both simple techniques to improve the quality of the course.

Note that participating in an online group involves a fair amount of time and effort for both staff and students, so it should *replace* existing course activities, not add to everyone's workload.

ACTIVITY 4B

Thinking about online discussion and communication

Remember to base your answers on the example course you chose in Activity 4A.

Do you, your teaching assistants and your students meet the three essential requirements outlined in section 2.2?

(a)   adequate access to networked computers?   ☐ yes   ☐ no

(b)   general computing skills, plus familiarity with e-mail and the Web?   ☐ yes ☐ no

(c)   technical support?   ☐ yes   ☐ no

If the answer to b) is no, do you think the opportunities afforded by online groups will justify the effort and time needed to meet those requirements? What sort of training is available? Could the acquisition of those key skills be counted as one of the learning outcomes of the course?

If the answer to c) is no, you will need to arrange support for the communication technology used – or choose a commercially-run system that meets your needs (see the Active*Guide for some options).

If the requirements are met, how would you see online discussions or communications improving your course? Some courses are open to multiple viewpoints and debates, while others teach facts and procedures and it may be hard to see any place for discussion. However, are there opportunities for small groups of students to work together on assignments, perhaps as competing teams? Would it be useful to assess the process as well as the outcome of collaborative work? See sections 4.1.6 and 5.3.2.

What benefits are you hoping to gain? What will be the benefits for your students?

What disadvantages can you foresee and how might they be avoided or managed?

How do you think your students will react to this use of technology?

4.1.2 Social aspects of online groups

Students working in online groups usually place great value on the advice and support they get from their peers. It also means that you are not the only person responsible (or available) to answer specific enquiries or provide comment. Answering these queries helps the students build a sense of community, and enables everyone to share their experience and knowledge. In addition, the feedback is available to the whole group and may well be of benefit to other students. You can use the discussions to identify areas of your teaching that need clarification, and to construct lists of FAQs with answers for subsequent classes.

The literature often makes much of the fact that online groups offer equality to those who are at a disadvantage in face-to-face tutorials – less assertive students, those speaking a second language and those who prefer to think before they answer. In an online group, everyone has the opportunity to take the time to marshal their arguments and present their views clearly. However, it is also true that:

- students who do well in face-to-face situations are often also confident online;
- some students, especially those who don't speak fluent English, may have trouble expressing their thoughts clearly;
- those who post their views first may place others in the frustrating situation of simply agreeing with them.

There are no easy solutions, but at least the opportunity for equality is present.

In groups that do not meet face-to-face, people are valued for their written contributions, and discrimination on the grounds of race, age or sex is minimized. It is possible in special circumstances for people to use a pen name that does not give any clues to their identity, although much of their character will be apparent to a careful reader through their writing. However, the use of completely anonymous messages should be avoided at all costs since it leads to confusion and lack of trust.

The effects of online groups on student motivation are complex. If the start is poorly managed and nothing seems to be happening initially, students will not be motivated to continue participating and useful discussions may never develop. Conversely, if the group generates too many messages then students will not have time to read and respond reflectively, and participation may become superficial. These issues are really your responsibility, since you must structure the tasks, facilitate the discussions and set the size of the group(s) – advice on this is given in sections 4.2 and 4.3.

The impact of people's real lives on their study is often acutely felt in online learning groups, particularly those comprising non-traditional students who are older, part-time, working (or not) and have family commitments. Their other responsibilities often affect their ability to participate, and they may 'disappear' for a while until their situation sorts itself out. You (and the other students) need to be sensitive to these problems, and ensure that absences are noticed and followed up – the longer a student is absent, the harder it is for them to 'reappear' without support and encouragement. A phone call is usually the most appropriate means of contact, especially if personal problems need to be discussed.

Generally, peer support extends beyond the academic to the social. Most online learning groups have forums in which the participants can chat about topics other than course-work, while in others it is acceptable to mix messages about work with social interaction. Messages providing support, advice or sympathy – as well as news, chit chat and jokes – provide an essential human link for learners who are physically isolated from each other. You should encourage the development of this social dimension to help transform a group of students into a learning community.

Learning Networks/Communication Skills

http://www.gla.ac.uk/services/tls/JISC/lincs.htm

This JISC-funded research project explores the characteristics of current communication media and defines the communication skills required in their educational use. As well as practical guidelines, the final report includes case studies and a set of narratives dealing with key emergent themes across educational contexts and technologies.

ASTER: assisting small-group teaching through electronic resources

http://cti-psy.york.ac.uk/aster/

This TLTP3-funded project aims to establish, validate and disseminate a corpus of good practice and expertise on the use of communications and information technology for small-group teaching. It has published reports that survey current practice in the humanities, sciences and social sciences.

4.1.3 Collaboration in online groups

Collaboration in an online group covers a spectrum of activities, ranging from academic discussion, through working together on an assignment, to forming the group, deciding the task and its assessment criteria. This continuum represents a shift in the balance of power and responsibility from you to your students, from guided learning to student-centred learning. It is beyond the scope of this section to do more than highlight some of the issues, so further reading is recommended – see the references at the end of this chapter.

There are fundamental differences in the communication that takes place in face-to-face and online groups (see Table 4.1), and you will need to be sensitive to these.

Discussions conducted online using text messages are very different to those held face-to-face. Text lacks all the social cues that we use in conversation – the non-verbal

Table 4.1   *Comparing face-to-face and online communication*

Face-to-face group	Online group
Channels of communication Uses a rich mixture of speech, delivery, posture and other body language to convey meaning and emotion. The speakers can adjust what they are saying in response to verbal and non-verbal feedback from the listeners.	**Channels of communication** Uses written text only, so meaning and emotion can only be conveyed by the writing skill of the authors. The authors must 'expose' themselves since they cannot get any feedback on what they say until it is too late to modify or 'unsay' it.
Mode of communication Synchronous, with all participants physically present at the same time. It is possible to have multiple discussions simultaneously. Participants have to 'think on their feet' as they develop their argument and respond to comments and criticisms immediately.	**Mode of communication** Asynchronous, with participants choosing their own time and place. The text style is likely to be informal and closer to speech than written prose. Messages can be carefully thought through, then edited and re-edited before they are posted.
Social cues to communication Participants are aware of the relative social status of the other participants, especially those who have greater power such as a tutor, expert or manager. There are also gender issues to be aware of.	**Social cues to communication** Many of the cues to social status are absent, so some social levelling is experienced.
Turn-taking It is possible to interrupt a speaker, or to ignore interruptions and dominate a debate. If you wait your turn you may not get to speak at all. You can also choose to avoid saying anything unless specifically asked.	**Turn-taking** There is no need to wait your turn since you can contribute as much and as often as you like. Your responses can be spontaneous or carefully thought-out. If you choose not to contribute, your absence is more easily checked.

feedback and body language that we use to judge the listener's response to what we are saying as we are saying it. This means that you take a risk when you post a message containing your opinions or ideas in an online group – you open yourself to potentially negative replies. What if there is no response at all? Does that mean your opinion is worthless, or that everyone agrees, or that they are all too busy to respond?

The absence of social cues and feedback also means that it is easier to over-react and say things that would not be said face-to-face. This can rapidly lead to heated exchanges known as 'flaming', which can disrupt the discussions and demotivate other students if left unchecked. You need to be aware of how quickly these 'slanging matches' can flare up, and extinguish them quickly with a private message reminding the students of the discussion's ground rules (see section 4.1.7).

Online groups need to build a sense of trust and shared purpose in order to minimize these risks and encourage open discussion. Fostering the development of a learning community in which the opinions of all participants are valued is one of the hardest tasks facing you. (Guidelines on this are provided in section 4.3 on facilitating online groups.) However, it is clear that all participants must abide by ground rules that encourage constructive criticism and peer support, otherwise students may simply opt out of the group if they feel threatened or ignored.

Working collaboratively with other students also has other effects on motivation. Being part of a group working together on an assignment creates a sense of responsibility to 'do one's best' and 'not let the others down'. On the other hand, active members of a group may resent doing 'more than their fair share' if they perceive that other members of the group are not 'doing their bit'. Dealing with these tensions and responsibilities is one of the key skills that working with others develops, and in some cases the process can be more important than the assignment itself.

In many cases, the online group will need to be split into much smaller groups to work together on assignments – the ideal size for these is between four and six people. Three or less may not create sufficient interaction, especially if one person does not participate much. Seven or more can create too much interaction and make it difficult to assign tasks. One problem for the tutor is how to form these groups. Letting the students choose their own groups presents many practical and social difficulties, and the process can be lengthy and divisive. Randomly chosen groups are acceptable, although many tutors may wish to adjust the results to ensure that each group has a mixed ability range.

CBCGW: Computer-based Collaborative Group Work

http://collaborate.shef.ac.uk/

This TLTP3-funded project is evaluating educational strategies to make use of learning technologies, as well as the learning technologies themselves. The Web site has many useful links organized into categories as well as a list of case studies (http://collaborate.shef.ac.uk/casebase.htm).

ALN: The Web of Asynchronous Learning Networks

http://www.aln.org/index.htm

This informal organization of educators is funded by the Sloan Foundation to 'make it possible for any person in the United States to learn at anytime and anyplace, in a subject of his/her choice'. The ALN publishes a journal, a freely accessible online magazine and holds face-to-face conferences. It also hosts online discussions about issues relating to Asynchronous Learning Networks.

ACTIVITY 4C

Shifting towards collaborative and student-centred learning

There are several dimensions to collaborative learning identified by McConnell (1994) such as the level of course structure imposed or the locus of assessment. Your position along these dimensions depends on the type of teacher you are, your students, your institution, the course level and the academic discipline.

Thinking about the example course you chose in Activity 4A, mark your current position on the central lines in Figure 4.1 to indicate the balance.

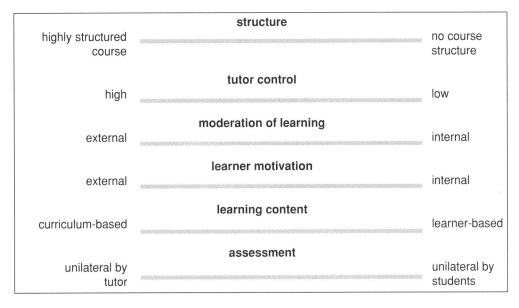

Source: McConnell (1994)

Figure 4.1   *Dimensions of collaborative learning*

If the positions you marked are predominantly towards the left, think about how the use of online discussions might move some of them to the right. Are your students prepared for this, and how might you support them in the process of becoming more self-managed?

Could the online discussions themselves be used to facilitate and support the process by starting with tightly defined tasks and gradually relaxing the degree of control and shifting responsibility towards the students?

What sorts of collaborative activities might be appropriate to your course? How do these relate to the learning outcomes of the course? Are there tasks that would work well with pairs of students or small project groups? Could their results be shared with the rest of the group as an online presentation? See also section 3.2.1.

Read this online resource by Paulsen. It is an excellent summary that briefly describes a wide range of techniques to provide inspiration and get you thinking about the possibilities.

Paulsen, M F (1995) The Online Report on Pedagogical Techniques for Computer-mediated Communication (online) NKI Electronic College of Computer Science

Available from http://www.hs.nki.no/~morten/cmcped.htm

Create a short document that links the course's learning outcomes to the activities planned for the online group. Add estimates of how much time you think they will take you to organize and manage and your students to complete.

4.1.4 The use of roles in online groups

You might want to encourage group members to adopt roles and responsibilities so that everyone is clear about who does what. For example, the 'chairperson' summarizes discussions and ensures that work progresses as planned, while the 'presenter' collates and formats everyone's work. All members need to be 'researchers' who find relevant resources, although individuals may agree to investigate particular issues. The role to avoid at all costs is that of 'leader' who is only responsible for controlling and directing the work of others, since that negates the essence of collaboration – 'working together'. See section 5.3.2 for a relevant case study by Buckner and Morss (1998).

In an ideal world, each group would be a model of equality, with each student switching seamlessly between roles as the need arose. Perhaps experience will allow students to work towards this goal, but in the initial stages the adoption of roles will clarify decision making and facilitate the successful and timely completion of the assignment. This success is a major motivational factor for students, and you should not lose sight of this even if you regard the collaborative process as the true learning objective.

4.1.5 Making decisions in online groups

One major argument in favour of clearly defined roles is the difficulty that online groups have when making decisions. The slow response times, sometimes measured in days, combined with the need to hear everyone's opinion, discuss the options and finally agree, means that the process can take forever – or at least seem that way! Issues that could be resolved in minutes in a face-to-face meeting can take weeks – and the process can be very frustrating and demotivating, as well as eating into the time and effort available to actually carry out the assignment.

A 'chairperson' can speed the decision-making process by setting out a clear schedule. For example, on Monday the chairperson might post a message saying, 'We need to decide X by next Monday, please post your views on this by Wednesday, read and respond to these over the weekend and cast your vote by Monday.' The assumption here is that all members of the group can and will access the online system three or more times a week. The dangers are that members whose other commitments mean they are unable to do this will be cut out of the process and that the tight schedule will lead to inadequate discussion and hasty decisions. Groups will need to find their own balance between speed, quality and inclusion.

It may be that groups will need to determine their own expectations on access and participation. For example, all members may agree to access the system at least once during the week and once at the weekend.

4.1.6   Assessing participation

The simplest and most mechanistic approach to assessment is to set criteria that the students must meet, such as posting five or more substantial messages. The software may make it easy for you to verify these details by displaying all the messages sent by any selected student. This may be acceptable if active participation in the discussions is a course requirement but is not assessed.

A marked assessment of the contribution made by a member to the group is much more complex, since the quantity of messages needs to be balanced against the quality of their content. You may not be in the best position to assess this either, since each student will have his or her own equally valid view. Allowing students to contribute to this assessment is another step towards student-centred learning, and using peer assessment in this way can be a powerful and sometimes uncomfortable learning experience for them. You could require them to write a reflective essay about what they have learnt from the discussions and form small groups that briefly discuss and assess each other's essays. See Figure 5.3 for a proforma for reflecting on teamwork.

Another option might be to give each student 20 points to split between the other students as they decide, depending on how they viewed their contribution to the group's activities, and send these marks in a private message to you. You would collate the marks and assign grades. It can be argued that quantitative assessment of this type is inappropriate for online groups, and that the only valid measure of learning is that internal to each student.

Section 5.3.2 also discusses the assessment of collaborative work and online discussions.

ACTIVITY 4D

How to assess participation

Some form of assessment is vital to encourage participation in online groups, otherwise it will be seen as an easily avoided optional workload. How can you match this assessment to the learning outcomes of your course? See section 5.2.1.

Will the activities and tasks in the online group produce essays, presentations or project work that can be assessed in the usual way? Will you also assess the process?

Will you simply assess participation by the number of messages posted by each student, provided their 'value' meets defined criteria that weed out insubstantial responses? Is this a pass/fail requirement or will a grade be assigned to each student based on their contributions? The latter is tricky, since the value of a message depends on its relationship to other messages posted by other students.

Is it practical or desirable to get the students to assess each other's work? Small groups of three or four could comment on each other's work, identifying strong and weak points prior to a final update and submission. Students can learn a lot by seeing the different arguments, interpretations and writing styles used by their peers.

Update the document you created in Activity 4B to include details of assessment methods, draft assessment criteria and an estimate of the time needed to assess each student.

4.1.7 Learning to learn online

It is not only tutors who are unfamiliar with what it is like to learn in an online group – many students will also find it a new and worrying experience. How does it work? What are they expected to do? How can they get the most from it? You should provide guidance on the social and learning skills that the students are expected to acquire – possibly as part of an initial training session in the use of the software. You may want to show your students Table 4.1 to highlight the differences between communication in face-to-face and online groups.

The ground rules for the forum should spell out such things as:

- The standard of writing expected. Is it formal and academic or relaxed and chatty? Should spelling errors be corrected or is it acceptable to 'typ quicly so long asits readable'?
- The length of messages. Online groups should be like a debate rather than a sequence of monologues, so essay-like messages should be discouraged unless that is what is specifically required.
- The content of messages. Should all messages remain 'on topic' or is some social chit chat allowable?
- The frequency of access. Two or three times a week is realistic, although short bursts of daily use may be possible.
- Rules about behaviour. These will typically forbid offensive, sexist or racist comments and insist that all criticism is positive and academic, never negative or personal.

On a deeper level, you should encourage all participants to post replies that take the debate forward instead of simply agreeing or disagreeing. Ideally, all participants should be leading each other towards a richer understanding of the topic under discussion. Skilled facilitators will lead the way by example, hoping that the students will adopt a similar approach as they gain in experience.

ACTIVITY 4E

Setting the ground rules

Create a document that clearly sets out the ground rules that you think are appropriate for your course and your students.

4.2 Structuring online seminars

Unstructured face-to-face discussions are seldom an effective seminar technique, although they do provide the freedom for unforeseen issues to emerge. As groups get larger, the need for some type of structure to the discussion increases. There are many resources available to guide tutors on face-to-face techniques, but how do these translate to online seminars?

Table 4.2 *Structures in face-to-face and online groups*

Face-to-face group	Online group
Rounds: everyone takes a turn to speak their questions, statement or opinion. Contributions tend to be quite short, since only a few minutes are usually allocated to this type of 'warm up' activity	**Rounds:** these work well online – all participants post a message containing their question, statement or opinion by a specified date. Contributions can be longer than those in a face-to-face session, or can be kept deliberately short. Students do not have to face the pressure of 'it's my turn next and I've got to say something clever!'
Buzz groups: sub-groups of three or four students discuss a topic for a short while. This can be a very quick and spontaneous activity used to break up a lecture and get the students talking about its content, possibly as a prelude to a quick question and answer session	**Buzz groups:** in an online group, the lag between message and response means there is no 'buzz', plus the total number of messages generated by the group can be overwhelming if students attempt to read them all. This technique is much better face-to-face
Pyramids: pairs of students discuss a topic, then form into fours or sixes to develop their ideas and arguments, before presenting them in a plenary session	**Pyramids:** again, this technique works much better face-to-face because it relies on negotiation and rapid feedback. The use of syndicates is a better alternative
Syndicates: sub-groups of students work on the same task (or related tasks) and present their outcomes in a plenary session	**Syndicates:** these can work well online provided each subgroup has its own private forum. Their results can be posted in a public forum accessible by all students
Fishbowls: most of the participants observe a discussion between a small sub-group, but do not contribute to it. The idea is that these 'listeners' learn by following the debate. It may be allowable for a listener to replace a 'speaker' if they request it	**Fishbowls:** this technique can work very well online, since it encourages a small volume of carefully-argued messages that can be read and re-read. The listeners may be able to debate the fishbowl in a separate forum, thus opening out the discussion
Brainstorms: the group attempts to solve a problem by rapidly creating a list of possible ideas, and then evaluates and criticizes them afterwards to determine which ideas might be potential solutions	**Brainstorms:** the initial 'idea generation' phase can work very well online, but making decisions about them as a group is much more problematic, unless some simple voting system is used
Organized debates: participants adopt a role in a scenario and argue a case from that position, regardless of their actual opinion. Examples include simulations of official enquiries, historical events and business meetings	**Organized debates:** this can be a very effective online technique provided everyone enters into the spirit of the scenario. It is even possible for participants to be identified by a pseudonym, so that their real identity is unknown

Some seminar techniques are actually easier and more effective online, while others are inappropriate. One of the crucial factors is time: online seminars can last for weeks, but the lag between a message and its reply can be days. Privacy is also an issue: it may be possible to split the group into smaller units, but often all participants can read every message if they choose. Bearing this in mind, some of the possible techniques are shown in Table 4.2.

A less structured debate that flows freely from topic to topic is possible, but usually requires a skilled tutor to moderate and facilitate the discussions. If the students are engaged in the debate and find it useful, the time and effort needed to participate will be seen as worthwhile. Success breeds success, and the forum will acquire its own momentum that only requires a light touch from you to continue. Practical advice on facilitation skills is given in section 4.3.

Paulsen, M F (1995) The Online Report on Pedagogical Techniques for Computer-mediated Communication (online) NKI Electronic College of Computer Science

Available from http://www.hs.nki.no/~morten/cmcped.htm

This document, already referred to in Activity 4C, lists a wide range of techniques and activities that can be supported by online communications. Note that this document is shareware and that the author requests you mail him a modest sum if you find it useful.

4.3 Facilitating online groups

Your facilitation skills play an important role in the success of your online discussion group. Good facilitation encourages interest, engagement and active debate, while poor facilitation can lead to rapid failure. This section provides practical advice on planning for success.

Other important facilitation skills obviously include the knowledge and expertise that you bring to the discussion. Good teaching and interpersonal skills are also needed, such as clear expression of ideas, enthusiasm, patience and the ability to draw people out and understand their viewpoint.

ACTIVITY 4F

Thinking about your role as a facilitator

In the diagrams in Figure 4.2, T represents you, the tutor, and S represents a student. Look at each of the diagrams and think about what they mean in terms of:

- the types of structure implied and the activities they can support;
- your power relationship with your students;
- developing your students' interpersonal skills;
- promoting independent learning;
- encouraging a deep approach to learning and metacognitive skills;
- your workload in facilitating the online group.

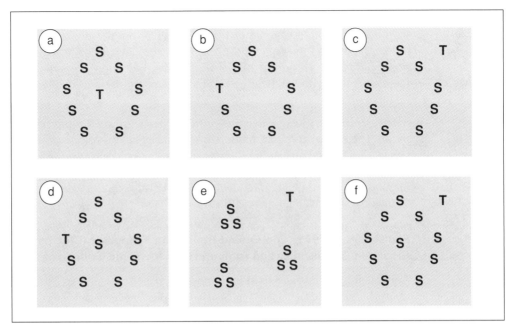

Figure 4.2   *Power relationships in online groups*

Which of these structures might you wish to use? Can you see them as a dynamic system, shifting in response to the tasks and circumstances of the moment? Which structures would you favour?

If the students are distance learners who will not meet during the course, it is an excellent idea to organize a face-to-face event before the online discussions begin. One reason is to ensure that everyone understands how to use the software, but an important secondary motive is for everyone to meet socially and be able to put faces to names. You might devise tasks related to the course that require the students to work together in small groups, and should allow plenty of time for informal contact during lunch and tea breaks.

If a face-to-face meeting is not possible, you should consider starting the online discussions with a structured task that gets everyone involved and contributing, for example by using syndicates. You should also ensure that there is a social forum for the students to use if they wish.

One of the problems that students may experience with online discussion groups is that they are not sure what type of social space it is and therefore what behaviour is appropriate. You can help them by using familiar words and concepts to label forums that not only define their function but also the type of message that is appropriate to each. An example is given in Table 4.3.

Table 4.3

Forum name	Function	Message type
seminar room office coffee bar	academic organizational social	formal academic debate informal, course queries informal chat

The start of an online discussion is a crucial time since it sets expectations. Make sure that the purpose of the online discussion is explicitly stated, along with its duration, milestone dates, expected outcomes and method of assessment. This may take the form of a printed study guide, which could also provide information about the course's structure, activities, procedures and resource materials as well as any relevant technical information and contact numbers. Alternatively, this could be published on the Web or sent to each participant as a file attached to an e-mail.

Beware of over-organization or proposing an over-complex structure, since you will inevitably need to be flexible as the discussions develop and flow. Your role is essentially to guide the discussion to a successful conclusion in the time available, restating and refocusing on the objectives if needed.

It may be possible to arrange for an invited expert to join the discussions for a few days, so they can respond to selected messages and answer questions from the students. This can help to liven up a group suffering from mid-session lethargy!

It is a good idea to start with a non-crucial task so that there is a week or so to sort out any access problems before the real work begins. For example, you could ask all the students to post a short note about themselves and also respond to a question – just enough to ensure that everyone can access the discussion and send messages.

You should encourage all students to participate, while recognizing that some may prefer to just follow the debate. Students who dominate the discussion could be gently requested via private e-mail to hold back a bit and wait for others to respond – you don't want to discourage active engagement, after all. Similarly you can e-mail non-participants, asking them if they have any views on the topics discussed and encouraging them to post them.

It is easy to offend someone with an ill-chosen phrase or a misunderstood attempt at humour. You should always be aware of the tone and content of your messages and strike a balance between informality and authority. Perhaps a good ideal to aim for is the 'knowledgeable friend'. If a student posts an inappropriate message, contact them privately via e-mail and suggest they post a clarification – don't be too authoritarian unless the circumstances demand it.

If someone makes a good point, acknowledge it with an open-ended reply or question that invites further comment and other views. You can also recognize several people's contributions by summarizing and weaving them together. This also refocuses the discussion, identifies unifying themes or conflicting views and can encourage further debate. However, do allow two or three days before responding so that other students have a chance to comment first – you should avoid dominating the discussions.

As more courses adopt these methods and students become familiar with participating in online discussions, you might hope that they will take their experience of good facilitation and start to facilitate the discussions themselves. It may be that you can encourage this behaviour by suggesting that a student takes that responsibility for the discussions around just one topic, maybe one that they had initiated. The aim is to develop their meta-cognitive skills as they compare, contrast and synthesize the multiple viewpoints presented.

At the end of the time available for the online discussions, be sure to finish by posting a message that thanks all the participants for their contributions and lets them know what happens next (if anything). You may also want to briefly identify the main topics covered and any conclusions reached.

This is also a good time to e-mail a questionnaire to gain feedback on the students' experience, as well as technical and administrative issues. While most questions may simply ask for ratings on a scale of 1 to 5, you might also require the students to write a short reflective essay on their personal experience and the learning that has taken place.

✍ ACTIVITY 4G

Developing your facilitation strategy and tactics

Download these three papers from the Internet and read them. Note that the first one requires you to have the Adobe Acrobat reader on your PC – see the Active*Guide for details of how to download and install this free software.

Green, L (1998) Playing Croquet with Flamingos: A guide to moderating online conferences (online) Ontario, Canada. Office of Learning Technologies

Available from http://www.emoderators.com/moderators/flamingoe.pdf

An excellent introductory booklet (in Adobe Acrobat format) for anyone thinking of using online conferencing, Well written, clear and to the point, this is the paper to read first. Green leads the reader through the entire process of creating and managing a conference, introducing the fundamental concepts and issues as she goes.

Rohfeld, R W and Hiemstra, R (1995) Moderating Discussions in the Electronic Classroom (online) Syracuse University. First published in Berge and Collins (1995)

Available from http://www.emoderators.com/moderators/rohfeld.html

This is another useful guide giving advice on how to set up and run an online conference. It pays particular attention to the planning stages and emphasizes the need for clear guidance for students on how to use this new medium. It also includes a number of techniques for 're-energizing the conference during periods of low activity' and has a useful bibliography.

Paulsen, M F (1995) Moderating Educational Computer Conferences (online) NKI Electronic College of Computer Science. First published in Berge and Collins (1995)

Available from http://www.emoderators.com/moderators/morten.html

This paper starts with a recommendation that 'moderators should identify their preferred pedagogical styles, based on their philosophical orientation, their chosen moderator roles, and their preferred facilitation techniques', and cross-references these to various moderator roles (eg, mentor or pace setter). Paulsen analyses the roles of the moderator in terms of their organizational, social and intellectual functions, and has guidelines that address each of these areas. This is really an extended piece of 'weaving' in which Paulsen has drawn together and summarized the ideas and advice given in the most influential papers and articles already published.

You should now have enough information to begin planning how you will set up and run the online group. Update the document started in Activity 4B to include:

- a list of the things you need to do or check before the start of the online group;
- how you will start the group and get your students online and involved;
- when and how much time you and any teaching assistants will spend managing the group;
- how you will conclude the group and provide feedback to the students;
- how you will evaluate the outcomes, benefits and costs of the group.

Collins, M and Berge, Z L (1998) The Moderators Page: Resources for moderators and facilitators of online discussion (online) Northern Arizona University

Available from http://www.emoderators.com/moderators.shtml

This is a first-rate resource that covers the practical, academic and technical aspects of setting up and managing online discussions. It includes many excellent papers that provide an overview as well as links to many Web resources and three bibliographies for further reading.

Berge, Z L (1996) The Role of the Online Instructor/Facilitator (online)

Available from http://www.emoderators.com/moderators/teach_online.html

This article lists the roles and functions of the online facilitator in computer conferencing and makes recommendations under four headings: pedagogical, social, managerial and technical.

Mason, R (1991) Moderating Educational Computer Conferencing, DEOSNEWS (online), 1 (19)

Available from: http://www.emoderators.com/papers/mason.html

Mason starts by presenting a few guidelines for online moderators; these cover their organizational, social and intellectual roles, and then presents an example of how good moderation skills might be applied in practice.

📖 **Feenberg, A (1989) 'The written world' in eds Mason, R and & Kaye, A R, _Mindweave: Communication, computers and distance education_, Pergamon, Oxford**

Available from http://www.emoderators.com/moderators/feenberg.html

This paper has had a considerable influence on later writings, in particular its ideas on 'Meta-communication and the art of weaving' and its table describing the contextualizing, monitoring and meta-functions of the moderator. Feenberg also analyses the online experience in a philo-sophical way, with ideas on discourse, identity and community.

4.4 How electronic communications can be used in learning and teaching

The previous sections have concentrated on the use of online discussion groups, but electronic communications can support a much wider range of learning and teaching activities.

4.4.1 Managing learning

The most elementary use is the management of learning. There are many administrative tasks that are quicker, cheaper and more convenient using electronic communications.

E-mail makes it easy to distribute information such as timetable changes, assignments or reminders to groups of students. You can quickly complete these tasks without clerical assistance, and the simplicity of this method means that you are more likely to use it frequently. In return, students can send information such as extension requests or change of address details either directly to you or to a course administration e-mail address.

More complex information can be sent as e-mail attachments. For example, students may be required to submit word-processed assignments this way. This has the advantage that the e-mail records the date and time it was sent, avoiding any argument, and it is easy for you to store copies of the assignments. The disadvantage is that you will either have to read the essays on-screen, or print them out – but this cost may be worth the convenience of electronic delivery.

Feedback on the assignment can also be returned electronically by simply replying to the original e-mail. You can easily keep a copy of this reply for future reference. Modern word-processors include annotation features, so you could return a copy of the original file with embedded comments – and this may be an argument in favour of on-screen reading and marking.

Course documents such as the syllabus, timetable, reading list and student handbook could also be distributed as e-mail attachments. However, to avoid any problems and ensure that all students have a readily accessible copy, these are probably still better distributed in printed or photocopied form. They also be made available on the Web, but again this cannot be the primary distribution route – or not for a few years at least!

4.4.2 One-to-one communication

At its simplest, this is a dialogue between you and a student, or between two students. You almost certainly have times at which students know that you are available in your office to provide support and discuss coursework. It may be much more convenient for students to phone you rather than come in person, especially if they are part-time or distance learners. Alternative technologies could include video-conferencing, especially if the system supports collaborative tools such as a whiteboard or remote editing of documents.

Students could also use e-mail to ask you course-related questions. The disadvantage of this approach is that the questions and replies are a private dialogue and are not shared with the rest of the class, even if they would have found them useful. It also puts the whole support burden on you and does not offer other students the opportunity to provide peer support. The use of a mailing list or online discussion forum is undoubtedly a better solution.

Students can and do make use of the phone and e-mail to provide peer support as a natural extension of the face-to-face support that has always occurred. The advantage of mailing lists and online discussion forums is that they extend the support available beyond each student's circle of friends to include the whole class. However, personal communication is still extremely important for providing emotional support and allowing private discussion about coursework that would not be possible or appropriate in a public forum.

4.4.3 One-to-many communication

You could set up a mailing list so that you can conveniently send e-mail messages to everyone in a group. This can function as an electronic notice board, so that messages contain changes to timetables, reminders about assignments, or alert students to a relevant television programme, for example. In this case, the mailing list may be set up so that only you can send messages.

If the students are also able to post messages to the list and have them copied to every member of the group, then the list can act as a rudimentary discussion forum. The advantage is that the only software needed is e-mail, but a consequent disadvantage is that it only takes a few active discussions to fill your e-mail in-box with messages each day. You will need to find out how to set up your e-mail software so that all messages from a list are automatically put in their own folder. This means that the lists do not swamp important messages and can be read later when convenient.

Another example of one-to-many communication is the use of video-conferencing to deliver a lecture. This can be used to allow a guest lecturer or expert to contribute to a course from anywhere in the world without requiring them to travel further than their nearest suitable video-conferencing facility. Ideally students should be able to ask the guest questions, so the session is more akin to a seminar or master class.

4.4.4 Many-to-many communication

The use of electronic communications to facilitate group discussions has already been extensively covered earlier in this chapter. Online discussion groups rely on the use of specialized software to create, store and organize messages. This software also controls access to the discussions and provides search facilities and the ability to see who has read each message. This level of sophistication is what separates them from mailing lists based on e-mail.

Other technologies for many-to-many communication include phone conferences and online chat systems, which are discussed in the next section.

4.5 Types of electronic communication

Electronic communication technologies can be grouped in a number of ways, but perhaps the most useful distinction is between:

- *synchronous communications* – such as a phone conversation, in which the participants are in contact at the same time; and
- *asynchronous communications* – such as e-mail, in which there is a significant delay between the transmission of a message and its reception.

Both of these are listed in Table 4.4. The first of these relies on having students who are able to participate at a specified time, which may present problems for part-time or distance learners, especially if they are scattered around the world in different time zones. Communication is rapid and informal, and decisions can often be reached quickly based on contributions from most participants.

In contrast, the second is ideal for part-time and distance-learners, since it allows them to participate at any time convenient to them. They can spend as long as they need composing their messages and a record is kept of messages and any replies. Communication is slower and usually more formal, and consensus decisions are notoriously difficult to achieve.

Table 4.4   *Synchronous and asynchronous modes of communication*

Mode	Face-to-face	Online: synchronous	Online: asynchronous
one-to-one	conversation	(phone) online chat	(fax) e-mail
one-to-many	lecture	streaming audio or video	audio or video files mailing list
many-to-many	debate	audio-conference video-conference chat room MOO	newsgroup discussion list

Note that many-to-many technologies will also support one-to-many communication, and these in turn will also support one-to-one interactions.

4.5.1 Phone

The telephone is the most ubiquitous and familiar electronic communication medium available, and can be an excellent choice for supporting part-time and distance learners. Most people have their own phone and are familiar with its use, so there are no training or technical support costs. Although it is a synchronous medium, the common use of answer-phones (or their digital equivalent, voice-mail) also allows it to be used asynchronously. Modern digital exchanges make it simple to set up three-way conferences (ie, between three phones) and larger conferences are possible with the assistance of the phone company.

The UK Open University has used multi-way phone conferences to support distance learners in remote areas for many years (George, 1998). Their experience is that it takes only a few minutes to get a tutorial group of eight people connected and that it works well provided everyone follows an agreed protocol about who can speak when. As the tutor and learners become familiar with the technique, a more natural style evolves, similar to that familiar from face-to-face meetings.

Its simplest use is for the management and support of learning – you phone individual students to remind them of deadlines, ask them about any problems, discuss plans and so on. Students can obviously also use the phone for peer support, and this can provide a valuable life-line for isolated distance learners. Its advantage in this case over text-based mediums such as e-mail is the social interaction and emotional feedback that conversation naturally provides.

If you decide to use the phone to manage and support learning, it is a good idea to have a set of guidelines that specify acceptable hours for contact and the time within which a response to an answer-phone message can be expected – you don't want to be disturbed by worried students ringing at inconvenient times!

ACTIVITY 4H

Conference calls

Find out if your institution's phone system supports three-way conference calls, and if it does, learn how to set one up – there may be all sorts of opportunities in which this feature may save time.

4.5.2 Fax

This is another low-tech solution that uses inexpensive, reliable equipment and needs no special skills. It could be used to complement phone calls by allowing documents to be copied quickly from one location to another. Documents could easily be shared and annotated by learners and tutors. The main disadvantage is the low quality of the printing. It is an asynchronous medium that can be used to distribute documents at off-peak times. Computers with fax-modems can be used to 'print' any document (such as a word-processed file or a spreadsheet) via fax to a list of phone numbers, minimizing the manual effort needed to distribute these documents to groups of students.

4.5.3 Electronic mail

E-mail is a simple and convenient way of exchanging text messages via the Internet. It is an asynchronous medium that allows messages to be sent at any time and read later at the recipient's convenience. Messages take no more than a few minutes to reach the other side of the world, so rapid responses are possible if the recipient is online and reads the e-mail as soon as it arrives. Here are some other useful features:

- text can be conveniently copied between e-mail messages and other applications;
- messages can be easily stored and organized for later reference;
- messages can easily be sent to multiple recipients or defined groups of people;
- it is possible to attach files (for example a word-processed document or spreadsheet) to a message, and e-mail is often used to distribute files in this way.

Most people use a desktop computer to read and send their e-mail, but a wide range of alternatives are possible. Common options include laptop computers, palmtop computers and handheld organizers which can be used to access e-mail from any location with a phone line. Alternatively, they can also be connected via a mobile phone from almost anywhere – an airport, building site, beach or mountain! Some mobile phones have e-mail built in, although their small keypads make sending messages inconvenient.

There are two basic types of e-mail; client-server and Web-based. The first type uses an *e-mail client* program installed on your computer to access an *e-mail server* via the Internet or office network. When you connect, the client retrieves copies of any new messages waiting for you and sends any messages you have composed. You can then disconnect from the server and read and reply to your e-mail at leisure, since they are stored on your computer's hard disk. This system is excellent for people using a modem and phone line, since it only takes a few minutes to exchange messages and minimizes call charges. People with a permanent Internet connection can set their client to check for new e-mail every few minutes – or at whatever frequency they find does not interrupt their work.

For people without a personal computer, Web-based e-mail may prove more attractive. You access your e-mail by using a Web browser to connect to your own account at one of the many sites that provide this service. A username and password are used to gain access to your e-mail account and ensure privacy. The disadvantage is that you need to stay connected while you read the messages and compose replies to them, so call charges are much higher for modem users. You also have no access to your messages unless you deliberately save them to disk. The advantage is that you can access your e-mail from any computer with an Internet connection, wherever you are in the world.

✎ **ACTIVITY 4I**

Using e-mail attachments

If you do not already know how, find out how to send and receive e-mail file attachments and practise exchanging a few documents with a colleague. You should also find out if it is possible to use your e-mail software to define groups of people so that it is easy to send a message to them all.

4.5.4 Mailing lists

While it is simple to send e-mail to groups of people, it is less easy for all members of a group to exchange messages. Every time someone joins or leaves the group, every member has to update their own list of e-mail addresses. Mailing lists automate this chore by providing a single e-mail address that will forward a copy of any message it receives to all members of the group or list. People can join or leave the list by sending an instruction to the computer running the mailing list service. A single computer can manage hundreds or even thousands of mailing lists. Popular programs used by educational institutions around the world include Listserv and Majordomo, and there are many others available. The differences between moderated and unmoderated mailing lists are shown in Figure 4.3.

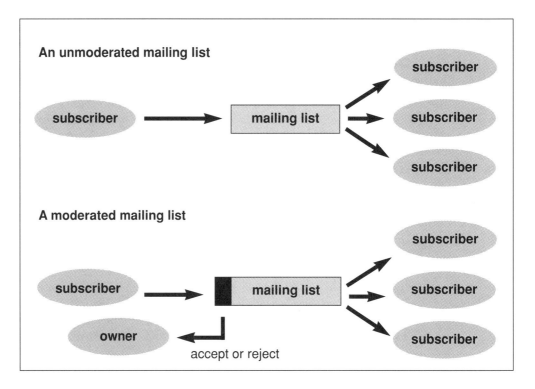

Figure 4.3 *Unmoderated and moderated mailing lists*

Each mailing list has an 'owner' who determines the features of the mailing list. Lists can be open for anyone to join, or membership may have to be approved by the list owner. Lists can be moderated by one or more people, who accept or reject messages posted to the list. This eliminates poor-quality contributions but requires continuous effort and can lead to arguments about editorial power. Alternatively, lists can be unmoderated and rely on their membership's good sense, although the owner always has the sanction of expelling any member.

Some systems keep an archive of messages, removing the necessity for individual members to do so. These archives are often accessible via the Web and can be browsed by date or searched by author, subject or keyword(s). File attachments allow mailing lists to be used to distribute documents or data to groups conveniently, quickly and cheaply.

Mailing lists are frequently used to support special interest groups, projects and classes. In the UK, the Mailbase service (http://www.mailbase.ac.uk) supports higher education and further education.

Some mailing lists get quite busy and generate many messages each day, which pile up in your e-mail inbox at an alarming rate. You can either leave the list and search its archives if you need to find out something, or develop a ruthless attitude and delete any messages that do not seem relevant at first glance. Mailing lists can waste a lot of time if you choose to do a lot of reading and replying.

ACTIVITY 4J

Joining Mailbase lists

Go to Mailbase at http://www.mailbase.ac.uk and browse by subject to locate two interesting-sounding lists. Check their archives for relevance and 'busyness', read the instructions on joining, and join. You can always leave the list if you find it generates too much e-mail or is not as interesting as you had hoped.

4.5.5   Conferencing

A range of terms is used to describe software that can be used to facilitate online discussions. They include computer conferencing, discussion lists and forums. There is also a wide spectrum of software systems:

- Text-only systems that are accessed by logging on to a remote computer and controlled by typing commands. Although functional, these systems are outdated and most students will find them unattractive and difficult to use.

- Web-based systems that are accessed using a Web browser. These may be functionally identical to the text-only systems but the mode of access and user interface make them a good choice. Some of these dedicated systems are very good and provide many advanced features.

- Web-based systems that form part of a managed learning environment that also provides controlled access to learning resources, online assessment and other facilities. The advantage of these is that the discussions are integrated into the online course, although the features may not be as sophisticated as those provided by a dedicated system.

● Client-server systems that use special software installed on the user's PC to communicate with a remote server that manages and stores the discussion forums. The advantage of these systems is that a local copy of each forum is kept on the user's PC so that the messages can be referred to offline, which minimizes the communication costs and is generally more convenient. The disadvantage is the cost of the software and the need for every user to have their own personal PC.

● Groupware systems have additional features that support collaborative work and decision making. They are often designed to support business activities and mostly have a price tag to match. They can be Web-based, use the client-server method or may even support both options.

All these systems are able to organize and display messages as 'threads', which consist of an original message plus any replies to it, as well as any replies to the replies, as shown in Figure 4.4.

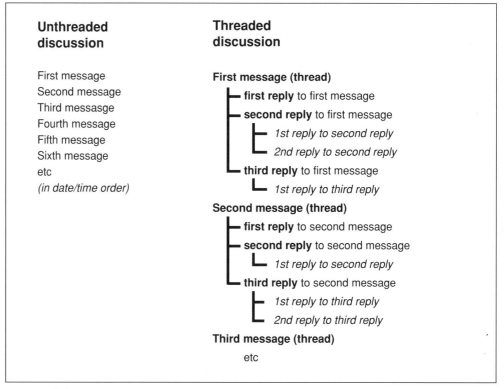

Figure 4.4 *Unthreaded and threaded discussions*

This technique enables many discussion threads to exist simultaneously, although only a few may be actively discussed by the group at any one time. Further messages can be added to older inactive threads at any time if there is something more to say. The advantage of a threaded discussion is that messages about a topic are grouped together, but there are also disadvantages. One is that the structure of a thread may become very complex and difficult to follow since the messages within a thread are not in date order and the sense of an ordered debate is lost. Another is the way in which messages drift off topic or refer to discussions in other threads.

For these reasons, unthreaded discussions in which all messages are shown in simple date order are conceptually easier to follow since they are similar to a face-to-face debate. However, threaded discussions allow interested participants to explore issues in depth without impeding the overall direction of the discussion. Participants need to be disciplined to use threads effectively:

- messages in a thread should be about the main topic;
- a new thread should be started if the topic changes;
- the description (subject line) of the first message in a new thread should accurately describe the topic.

Some systems allow you to choose between threaded and unthreaded modes.

4.5.6 Newsgroups

Newsgroups (also known as Usenet) allow millions of Internet users to discuss almost any topic with each other. There are over 30,000 newsgroups available, each devoted to a specific topic, ranging from the serious (cancer self-help) through the popular (TV shows) to the bizarre (stranger than you can imagine). Messages posted to a particular newsgroup are automatically propagated across the Internet via news servers, each of which takes its news 'feed' from several servers and acts as a 'feed' for others. Old messages are deleted after a few days, although a service called DejaNews keeps a permanent and searchable archive of most groups.

Both Netscape Communicator and Internet Explorer come with free software that can be used to access selected newsgroups and send messages to them. Alternatively, special-ized software that offers more sophisticated features can be used for that function. These include the ability to automatically filter out messages from selected people whose messages annoy you, or messages that contain specified words and phrases. This is useful, as newsgroups are the target of a great deal of 'get rich quick' and other 'spam' (unwanted messages).

From an educational perspective, the main problem is that newsgroups are open for anyone to read and post to. If the group uses a local news server, it can be instructed not to feed that newsgroup to any other servers, but it is still open to all users of that server. This is a shame, as otherwise they offer most of the features of threaded discussion lists.

DejaNews

http://www.deja.com/

Deja maintains an archive of newsgroup messages and enables you to search them by keyword or browse through hierarchical categories. It acts as the collective memory of Internet news-groups and can be used to find subjective advice on almost any topic.

4.5.7 Instant messaging and chat rooms

Instant messaging technologies such as ICQ ('I seek you') enable one-to-one communication. Whenever you are connected to the Internet, the software sends a message to a central server to say that you are online and checks to see if any of your friends are also online. If they are, it lets you know so you can send them a message, and if they respond you can have a typed conversation. Your friends are also alerted to your presence by the server, so they can also initiate a conversation. You define your list of friends by typing their unique ID numbers into the software; people who use this technology often include their ID in their e-mail signatures.

In an educational context, some students already use this to chat informally and discuss course issues with their peers. Distance learners could be encouraged to install the software, exchange IDs and connect to the Internet at predetermined times if they want to communicate in this way. Instant messaging can be integrated with other applications, such as one-to-one audio or video conferencing, so that richer forms of communication can be initiated and files or Web addresses exchanged.

Internet chat rooms use virtual spaces in which groups of people can 'talk' in real time by typing short messages to each other. However, everyone can hear (read) everything that is said in that space, and the effect of all these mixed-up fragmented conversations cascading down your screen can be very confusing for novices. Even worse, the need for fast typing means that grammar and correct spelling are discarded and replaced by cryptic abbreviations and jargon.

The name 'chat' is well chosen, since this is not a medium that favours reasoned debate. By the time you have typed your carefully worded paragraph to answer some point, the conversation will have moved on and your message will be a lengthy irrelevance. Paragraphs need to be split into short sentences so they are interleaved with the other messages. Students who are familiar with the medium may cope, but others will be left bewildered.

Instant messaging may well be useful to provide support for distance learners, but a phone call is a much richer and faster means of communication. Chat rooms may also be useful to provide some informal social contact for distance learners away from their discussion forum. In terms of education, however, more sophisticated chat-based environments called MOOs offer the only real benefits (see section 4.5.8).

ICQ

http://www.icq.com/

ICQ was the original instant messaging software service. The Web site has links to many categories of users and interest groups, lets you find out more about the uses of instant messaging, download their free software and sign up for your unique ID number.

Microsoft Network MSN Messenger

http://msn.co.uk/page/11-141.asp

Microsoft's software is tightly integrated with the latest versions of their other communication tools and services, such as Outlook Express, Netmeeting and Hotmail. However, note that all these instant messaging products are currently incompatible – for example MSN Messenger will not tell you about friends who use ICQ. You can find out more, download the software and register yourself.

America Online AOL Instant Messenger

http://www.aol.com/aim/home.html

This service currently boasts over 40 million users, based on AOL's huge number of subscribers. You can find out more, download the software and register yourself – you don't have to be an AOL subscriber to use this service.

4.5.8   MOOs and MUDs

MOOs and MUDs originated in the text-based adventure games that were popular in the early days of the Internet, before the Web evolved. Participants type instructions that move them around an imaginary world made of words – a series of connected spaces described in more or less detail. Objects (described) in these spaces can sometimes be examined (more description), picked up and used in the game. If two or more participants are present in the same space at the same time, they can see each other (read a description of the other's appearance) and talk to each other by typing messages.

Many people spent a great deal of time and inventiveness creating beautifully detailed worlds – these were often collaborative efforts by groups of friends who had only ever met in these textual spaces. Visiting these worlds, wandering around and interacting socially with the people you met there proved to be an addictive pastime for some.

MOOs and MUDs can be used in an educational context by providing spaces in which groups of students can communicate in real time. Being a touch-typist helps, although a casual attitude to spelling and grammar is also the norm. Messages are best kept very short, or split into small chunks, otherwise the flow of conversation moves on while you type a lengthy response. Educational spaces may have special features such as:

- special status for the tutor, who can 'shut everyone up' or allow free comment;
- a stage, which allows students to listen only to anyone standing on it and cut out comments from other students;
- a slide projector, which enables the tutor to show pre-prepared 'text slides';
- a tape recorder, which keeps a copy of all messages for later review and use.

There are also MOOs and MUDs with graphical interfaces – the spaces are represented by an image, and the participants by small icons. Messages appear as speech bubbles coming from these icons. These are interesting, but better for social than educational use. A further progression is 3-D virtual worlds, similar to many modern computer games, but inhabited by hundreds of real people whose presence is signified by animated realistic figures within the virtual world. These places are the closest the Internet comes to the futuristic cyberspace of science fiction films and novels, and their citizens relish their pioneer status on this new electronic frontier.

4.5.9   Video and audio files

Computers can be used to record and store audio and video as digital files (see sections 2.3.6 and 2.3.7 for further details). With appropriate hardware, software and experience, creating such files can be as easy as sending an e-mail and can be used as an alternative to typed messages. The files can be attached to e-mail messages sent to individuals or groups, or can be stored on a Web server so they can access them on demand.

The only disadvantage is that the files are much larger than text messages and will take longer to download. On the other hand, they may be much quicker to record than an equivalent typed message and are a much richer form of communication. They also offer real advantages in disciplines such as foreign languages and for students with dyslexia or impaired sight.

4.5.10   Streaming audio and streaming video

It is possible to use streaming media technologies to support synchronous one-to-many communication – in effect an Internet-based radio or TV broadcast. Potential applications include lectures by invited experts and reports from conferences or other events and locations. The disadvantages are the high level of technology needed, including special server software. The quality of the broadcast can be pretty low using standard Internet streaming technologies, so uses such as demonstrations of advanced surgical techniques rely on dedicated point-to-point high bandwidth network links or satellite broadcasts. Apart from the initial set-up costs, neither of these is as expensive as you might suppose and they do deliver the quality required. (See section 2.3.7 for details of streaming media technologies.)

 Real Networks

http://www.real.com

You can download the free RealPlayer G2 software from this Web site, find out more about the technology and access a wide range of streaming media broadcasts.

MBONE: Multicasting Tomorrow's Internet

http://www.savetz.com/mbone/

The complete text of a book published in 1996, so it is a little bit dated but contains a link to another Web site – http://www.mbone.com – that has the latest information and further links.

4.5.11   Video-conferencing and audio-conferencing

The simplest application of video-conferencing (VC) is as a video-phone which allows two people to see as well as hear each other. Low-cost cameras and advanced software make this just possible using a modem, but a faster Internet connection will greatly improve the quality of the sound and picture. Note that the video image is small and rather jerky. The software may also allow information to be shared in other ways, ranging from exchanging typed messages through a shared electronic whiteboard to remote control of applications. The latter allows both people to collaborate on editing a word-processed document, for example.

Microsoft NetMeeting, which comes free with the Internet Explorer Web browser, requires you to make the connection via one of its servers. This allows several people to join a virtual meeting in which everyone can see and hear just one person at a time. This is a limitation, but does enable activities such as online tutorials.

Video-conferencing software can also be used for audio-conferencing if the video image is not considered useful, the students do not have video cameras attached to their PCs, or if the Internet connection is simply too slow to support video. Audio and a shared white-board can be a very effective educational combination.

More expensive technology and communications are needed to hold a true online meeting with high-quality two-way video and sound. Many businesses use special VC equipment and digital ISDN phone lines to hold meetings between remote offices or with clients. The high cost of the equipment and calls is easily offset by the elimination of travel time and costs.

Educational institutions may have a central VC suite, but most only have room for a few people. It is much rarer to have a facility that can cope with groups of even 30 students which would allow activities like tutorials and presentations by invited experts. These busy people are much more likely to agree to participate if it involves an hour in a local VC suite rather than a day or more of travel. It also makes guests from other countries a realistic proposition, provided time zone differences can be worked around.

ACTIVITY 4K

Checklist for Chapter 4

1. Find out what types of communications technologies are available and supported by your institution. Ask your computing service or educational technology support unit, if you have one. They may be able to put you in contact with other staff who are already using them so you can find out about local issues and experience.

2. Can you make use of communications technologies to help you manage the learning? See section 4.4.1 for details of how this can provide immediate tangible benefits to both you and your students without requiring major changes to the course.

3. If you want to use communications technologies to support and facilitate learning and teaching, what are the learning objectives that these activities will address? How will these be assessed?

4. Given the investment in time and effort needed to create, manage and participate in such activities, which existing parts of the course will they replace? How will they be integrated with the remainder of the course?

5. How will these activities be evaluated? What criteria will be used to measure intangible benefits such as the development of interpersonal skills, effective use of C&IT and greater independent study skills?

References

Berge, Z L and Collins, M P (eds) (1995) *Computer-mediated Communication and the On-line Classroom in Distance Education*, Hampton Press, Cresskill, NJ

Bukner, K and Morss, K (1998) The importance of task appropriateness in computer-supported collaborative learning. *ALT-J*, **7**(1), pp 33–38

Cornell, R and Martin, B L (1997) 'The role of motivation in web-based instruction' in ed B H Kahn, *Web-based Instruction*, Educational Technology Publications, Englewood Cliffs, NJ

George, J (1998) 'Learning technologies network: implementing learning technologies: strategies and experience', keynote presentation at the SEDA biannual conference held at the University of Southampton, 7 April

Gibbs, G (1995) *Teaching More Students 3: Discussion with more students*, Oxford Centre for Staff Development, Oxford

Keller, J M (1983) 'Motivational design of instruction', in ed C M Reigeluth, *Instructional-Design Theories and Models: An overview of their current status*, Lawrence Erlbaum, Hillsdale, NJ

McConnell, D (1994) *Implementing Computer Supported Cooperative Learning*, Kogan Page, London

5 Assessing student learning

Assessment techniques have tended to lag behind the innovative teaching that has been taking place within higher education. Much of this is to do with the regulation concerning the validation of courses that governs the type and quantity of assessment allowed. This prevents, to some degree, an innovative approach to assessment. However, we are seeing increasing interest in how we can assess students to support the varied learning outcomes we are adopting in our teaching programmes. In this chapter we will discuss:

- the dilemmas we face as practitioners regarding assessment (5.1);
- the uses of technology in the assessment process – delivering tests, an aid to collaborative learning assessment, electronic portfolios, etc (5.3);
- how we deliver and manage computer aided assessment (5.3);
- the software we can use and some practical exercises to try out from the Active*Guide at http://www.clt.soton.ac.uk/activeguide.

5.1 Dilemmas of assessment

One dilemma is the tension that can exist between the various stakeholders in higher education assessment. The major players in the process are:

- The institution   is concerned with quality and accountability to government inspectors and prospective students (Quality Assurance).
- The tutor   is concerned with how well his or her programme went (evaluation/quality).
- The learners   want to know how well they are doing; what they need to do to improve (the learning process).
- The parents   as the cost of higher education increases, parents will have more voice in where their children study.
- The employers   want to know what people are able to do if they graduate in a certain subject, and how suitable the person is for the job.

On the face of it, these groups seem to fit together well. On closer inspection, however, we know that the institution is more concerned with grades to complete the pass/fail tables and that tutors are similarly concerned with this, as their performance will be judged accordingly. The learner, on the other hand, apart from supplying the grades to be recorded, has no say in the process at all. The employers, who increasingly need to know what skills a graduate has in a given subject, are making their voice heard by creating their own 'league tables' of universities from where they recruit graduates.

Another dilemma is that traditional assessment in higher education is predominantly *norm-referenced*, ie, an exam grade that shows how students compare with each other. Therefore, a student's grades could come within the top 5 per cent of their cohort (a good pass) or within the lowest 20 per cent of their cohort (a fail). Very often there is a system for restricting how many can receive top grades in order to preserve 'quality'. Criterion-referenced assessment, on the other hand, measures how well students have performed against given criteria, independently of their peers. This assesses what the student can do. *Criterion-referenced* assessment therefore reflects the competencies of students on particular skills (intellectual, practical or social). As competency-based education becomes more important with the need to develop lifelong learning skills, particular intellectual skills as well as generic key skills, criterion-referenced assessment may need to be addressed more coherently across all subjects.

There are discussions in the literature regarding the differences between *competence-based* and *performance-based* assessment. Both are a form of criterion-referenced assessment. Competence-based assessment will clarify the learning goals more accurately, so students can receive accreditation when they are deemed 'competent' in a given area. With performance-based assessment, students need to match their performance against the criteria specified. Such assessment asks not only for competence on a narrow range of skills, but also performance across a wide set of contexts (Hinett and Thomas, 1999).

A third dilemma, and similar to that above, is that the traditional 'bolt on' exam, based on the essay, may not be coherent with the changes we are making within our courses that encourage more independent, collaborative learning. We probably already notice that students' learning is not being assessed effectively by the traditional exam essay alone. Our external stakeholders (especially government inspectors and employers) will increasingly voice their concerns about this.

New learning and teaching methods therefore need new and innovative assessment methods that maintain quality, measure what is being learnt and are central to the learning process. Innovative assessment tends to reside in the area of formative assessment (ie, ongoing assessment) as opposed to summative assessment (final assessment). The major dilemmas of assessment outlined above refer mainly to the general rigidity of summative assessment procedures.

Pedagogical Frameworks and Action Research in Open and Distance Learning

Peter Goodyear, 1999, University of Lancaster

http://kurs.nks.no/eurodl/shoen/goodyear/index.html

An interesting article which, although not solely related to 'assessment', makes one think about it in the pedagogical design, because it is necessary to set up the most appropriate pedagogical framework within which to base the assessment.

5.2 Mapping learning and assessment

Before assessing students, we need to establish the learning outcomes. Learning outcomes stem from the aims of the course and clarify the goals expected of the students. The learning outcomes will then determine the kind of learning event and task(s) that can be set for students. The learning outcomes and tasks set by the tutor refer to the pedagogy (teaching) of the course, while the activity to complete the task and the assessment of the actual learning outcomes are within the realm of *learning*, as illustrated in Figure 5.1.

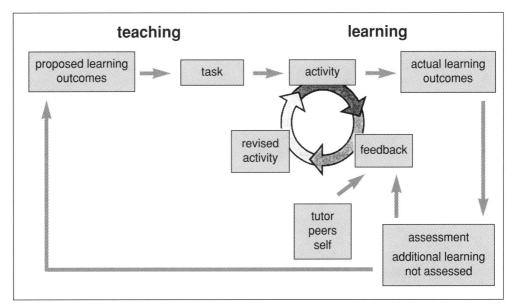

Figure 5.1 *Task-activity cycle*

Learning takes place in the activity loop, which is heavily affected by feedback from peers and tutors (and 'self' as a form of reflection). Within this model, assessment is firmly located within the learning cycle and provides some input for feedback. It will also feedback to the 'proposed learning outcomes' as the tutor evaluates the whole process.

The reflective process, therefore, as well as the 'end-product', can also be part of the assessment. Focus on the reflective process by giving students a proforma to work with. This activity (a reflective/reflexive journal) encourages independent learning and the ability of students to become reflective practitioners. Jolly and Radcliffe (Web site) used this with engineering students who were carrying out group project work. Students had to complete three questions:

1. *What happened?*   Record significant events.
2. *So what?*   Why the events were significant. If something went wrong, what was it, why did it go wrong and what were the consequences for the project? If nothing happened, how does it affect your progress?

3. *Now what?*   What do you do next? Issues arising out of last week's work, resolving unfinished business, solving problems.

These reflexive journals were then assessed by peers and tutor according to the following criteria: *diligence* (regular entries), *application* (using the reflexive sessions), and *development* (outcome as a result of the process).

Formative assessment, therefore, should be designed to play an active role in the learning process. Criteria need to be set for successful completion of the task, which can be set wholly by the tutor or through negotiation with students. Whichever method, it is important that students are thoroughly aware of the criteria and can work with them. This is important if they are expected to do any peer or self-assessment work. Encouraging peer and self-assessment is essential in developing reflective, independent learners. The assessment criteria are derived from the learning outcomes and indicate *how* and to *what level* the student should achieve the learning outcomes in order to pass the course (you may even want to further grade the criteria for commendations).

Make sure your assessment criteria reflect progression in students' skills. Consider what they should be able to do in particular skills across the years. Make students aware of this progression so they are also able to assess themselves and work towards the next level.

You will, however, be more restricted in your ability to alter summative assessment procedures at your institution, which are a formal assessment of a student's knowledge, skill and understanding. Check with your quality assurance handbook to determine how (if) you can make changes to assessment.

The Art of Assessing

Phil Race (1995)

http://www.lgu.ac.uk/deliberations/assessment/artof_content.html

This article first appeared in the SEDA publication *New Academic* and is now published by DeLiberations. It discusses the advantages and disadvantages of a variety of assessment procedures, with some tips for getting it right.

How to...

Lesley Jolly and David Radcliffe

http://mama.minmet.uq.edu.au/~radcliff/surfer/how-to.htm

Their neat site looks at various issues dealing with teamwork. For their use of reflexive journals, just follow the link.

5.2.1   Writing learning outcomes

The work of Bloom and Krathwohl (1956) and Krathwohl *et al* (1964) is an influential source of information upon which learning outcomes are based. Their taxonomy is divided into three overlapping domains: *cognitive*, *affective* and *psychomotor*. These domains have been used to create learning outcomes that are expressed using active verbs that indicate what the student will be able to *do* at the end of the learning event.

Cognitive learning (writing learning outcomes for cognitive skills)

This reflects knowledge and intellectual skills which the authors further break down into: *knowledge, comprehension, application, analysis, synthesis* and *evaluation*. A list of active verbs has been attached to these areas which you can use when writing learning outcomes; these are shown in Table 5.1.

Table 5.1

Cognitive Domain	Selection of active verbs for learning outcomes
1. **Knowledge** – ability to recall previously learnt material, know specific facts/ methods, procedures, know basic concepts/principles	define, label, recall, order, list, quote, match, state, recognize, identify
2. **Comprehension** – ability to understand the meaning of material, interpret charts/graphs, estimate future consequences implied in the data	describe, discuss, summarize, paraphrase, report, review, understand, explain
3. **Application** – ability to use learnt information in new situations/problem solving/solutions that have 'best answers', demonstrate correct usage of procedures, apply laws/theories to practical situations	assess, demonstrate, examine, distinguish, establish, show, report, implement, determine, produce, solve, draw, interpret, provide, use, utilize, write
4. **Analysis** – ability to identify component parts of knowledge, to understand its structure and composition, recognize logical fallacies in reasoning, make distinctions between facts and inferences	analyse, illustrate, discriminate, differentiate, distinguish, examine, question, infer, support, prove, test, experiment, categorize, write
5. **Synthesis** – ability to creatively apply knowledge to new areas, integrate new knowledge, write well argued paper/speech, propose research design to test hypothesis	compile, categorize, generate, negotiate, reconstruct, reorganize, revise, validate, organize, plan, propose, set up, write, substitute, initiate, express, compare, modify, design, create, build, devise, integrate
6. **Evaluation** – ability to judge the value of evidence/material for a given purpose	appraise, criticize, assess, argue, justify, defend, interpret, support, estimate, evaluate, critique, review, write

Levels 1–2 could be considered 'basic', levels 3–4 as 'intermediate', and levels 5–6 as 'advanced'. Most learning outcomes within higher education come from the cognitive domain. However, with increasing emphasis on group learning, lifelong learning and key skills, there is a renewed interest in including learning outcomes from the other domains.

Affective learning (writing learning outcomes for group work)

This kind of learning is reflected in attitudes towards tasks and working with others, eg the ability to be interested, attentive, responsible, support others, respect others, be a good listener and respond to the interactions of others. Many of these are interpersonal skills that are essential for group work and reflect the value held by the individual and the course programme. Some of the active verbs that could be used in this context are: supports, shares, responds, judges, joins, questions, praises, listens, argues, responds, challenges, integrates, enjoys, volunteers.

Psychomotor learning (writing learning outcomes for practical work)

This kind of learning demonstrates physical skills such as dexterity, coordination and manipulation that reflect either fine or gross motor skills. Some of the active verbs you could use in this context are: coordinates, balances, operates, handles (with confidence/skilfully), expresses, performs, calibrates.

It is also essential to map the most appropriate learning event to the learning outcomes – see section 3.2.1 for a list of learning events that support independent learning.

Developing Learning Outcomes

St Edward's University, Austin, Texas

http://www.stedwards.edu/cte/devlear.htm

This is an interesting site on developing learning outcomes with a link to information on Bloom's taxonomy.

5.2.2   Mapping types of assessment with skills assessed

Different learning outcomes lend themselves to different learning tasks and ultimately to different types of assessment. Below are some types of assessment, with an attempt at looking at some of the generic skills involved.

Exams (closed book)

- Ability to: interpret questions, address questions succinctly, write coherently at speed, recall from memory, time manage, think clearly under pressure.
- Measures: abilities above, product.
- Assessors: tutor and external examiner.

Exam (open book)

- Ability to: interpret questions, address questions succinctly, write coherently at speed, time manage, think clearly under pressure.
- Measures: abilities above, product.
- Assessors: tutor and external examiner.

Essay

- Ability to: interpret questions, address questions, undertake research (information handling skills – library, the Web), write coherently, prepare a presentation (word-processing, incorporating other media), formulate argument with supporting evidence, critically analyse and evaluate.
- Measures: abilities above, product, possibly self-reflection.
- Assessors: tutor, external, peer reviews (can put essays on the Web and ask for peer comments), self (student can assess own work/others' work prior to tutor – according to set criteria and then compare both comments for feedback).

Review (paper/book)

- Ability to: understand paper/book in depth, develop 'position' for the review, summarize findings, evaluate content, relate to other work where appropriate, write coherent analysis.
- Measures: abilities above, product, research skills.
- Assessors: tutor, external, peers (can put essays on the Web and ask for peer comments), self (student can assess own work/others' work prior to tutor – according to set criteria and then compare both comments for feedback).

📖 **Critical Reviews**

Steve Draper, University of Glasgow

http://www.psy.gla.ac.uk/~steve/resources/crs.html

Draper has written these guidelines for students of Psychology from his experience of marking student reviews.

📖 **Criteria for Assessing Oral Presentations**

Pat Maier, Centre for Learning and Teaching, University of Southampton

http://www.clt.soton.ac.uk/cltks/index.htm

Select 'Resources' for some key skills. This criteria sheet has been presented to students who can then modify it and use it for peer assessment. One particular group felt more comfortable assessing only the presentation skills of participants and not the content aspect, leaving this to the tutor.

Creating Successful Group Assignments

Georgeanne Cooper and Michael Sweet, University of Oregon

http://darkwing.uoregon.edu/~tep/assessment/groups.html

They also have a link to an article on Peer Evaluation. This file is in PDF format (Adobe Acrobat). To find out more about Adobe Acrobat files check the Active*Guide.

A Series of Assessment Criteria Checklists

http://www.lgu.ac.uk/deliberations/seda-pubs/Donaldson.html

Reproduced by DeLiberations with permission from the authors: Donaldson, A and Topping, K (1996) from 'Promoting peer assisted learning amongst students in higher and further education', SEDA Paper.

✍ ACTIVITY 5A

Skills and assessment

Look at these other types of assessment you can use. Can you determine what abilities could be assessed, what is measured and who the assessors are?

- Multiple-choice questions (MCQs) (see 5.3.1).
- Exhibitions.
- Oral presentations.
- Posters.
- Practicals/field work.
- Group projects.
- Individual projects.
- Viva.
- Portfolio.

Now, think of a course you are working with currently:

- What are the aims of the course?
- What are the learning outcomes?
- What are the assessment criteria for the particular learning outcomes?
- Which form of assessment would be a best measure of success?
- Who will assess?

5.3   Computer aided assessment

Technology can be used in assessment in a variety of ways, as seen in Figure 5.2. In this section we will concentrate on how the technology can be used, the types of assessment supported best by technology and the software that is available to implement it.

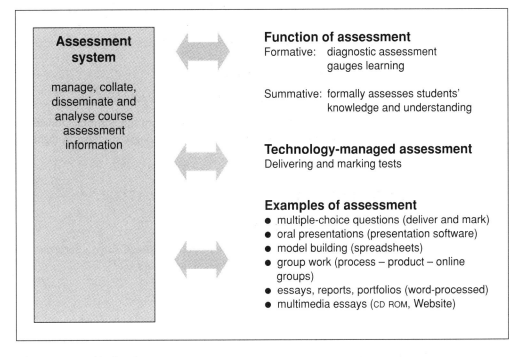

Figure 5.2 *Technology in assessment*

Technology can be used in formative testing, providing an excellent way of supporting student learning. Once a test is made available to students, they can take it repeatedly, learn from the feedback, and efficiently monitor their progress. This can all take place without extra effort on the part of the tutor (see section 5.3.1). This is the area most covered by papers on 'computer assisted assessment' (CAA).

In addition to these objective tests, technology can be used in collaborative learning environments as the medium of assessment (see section 5.3.2). This is proving a very fruitful area for assessment: as with computer mediated conferencing for example (or even e-mail discussions), there is a permanent record of the discussions (see section 4.1.6).

Students' work that is presented electronically is also being used increasingly as part of the assessment process. Some examples of different kinds of assessment that can be used with technology are shown in Table 5.2.

Finally we will look at how technology can be used to deliver and manage assessment (see section 5.3.3).

Table 5.2

Essay or reports	Technical drawings	Model building	Oral presentation	Develop taxonomy	Develop learning package	Portfolios
Word-processed text Can integrate multimedia components into word-processed documents Hyper-linked text for the Web	Using CAD programmes	Create a spreadhseet Illustrations through CAD packages	Using presentation software Delivery via OHP acetates or the PC	Create a database	Using the Web, spreadsheets or authoring software such as ToolBook	Using word-processors, the Web or authoring software

5.3.1 Objective tests for computer assisted assessment (CAA)

An objective/closed question test is the main type of test used with CAA. An objective test poses 'questions' where there is only one correct answer from a set of options or alternatives. Some examples of these tests are:

- *MCQs.* A selection of possible answers are offered to the question. Students select the one they think is correct. There should be only one correct answer.
- *Labelling images.* Tutor provides the images and the labels that the student then has to drag to the correct position.
- *Rank ordering.* Students are expected to use their knowledge to sequence events, determine cause and effect, etc – any task where the order is important. Again this can be achieved by the tutor providing the elements of the sequence that students are supposed to order.
- *Gap filling.* This is particularly used in language learning where texts contain gaps with a number of missing words that students select from to complete the text. This is ideal for testing verb tenses, a particular register for vocabulary, preposi-tions, etc.

These tests are not generally well received in the higher-education community as they appear to assess rote and surface learning. This can indeed be the case if they are not well written. These deceptively simple tests take a great deal of skill for the tester and the person being tested.

Writing MCQs

The popular misconception of MCQs is that they are all of the true/false type and, depending on how difficult they are, can either seem like a trivial quiz or be so difficult that the student can do nothing but guess.

Basic principles for writing MCQs

The MCQ comprises two parts: the stem (the question or statement) and the options/alternatives (the possible answers).

The stem should be clearly stated with no extra detail that can lead to both increased reading time and confusion. Some of the things to avoid using are:

- Jargon words unless they are an essential part of the stem.
- Negative words, unless it is necessary – then highlight them by underlining or using capitalization to draw students' attention to them.
- Conditional sentences unless really essential.
- Clues that point to the answer, eg, the grammatical construction in the stem might match one of the options better, or the choice of words in the stem may appear in the correct option only.
- Culturally biased statements that handicap students from other cultures, eg, using sports like cricket, football, horse racing, etc. These also tend to be mainly male sports.

The options should:

- Be equally plausible.
- Be of similar length. One more detailed option might indicate that it is the correct answer.
- Not use words/phrases that have been used in your lecture unless all the options contain that word/phrase.
- Not have *one* option (very often the correct one) that grammatically matches the stem, or uses the same words/phrases that appear in the stem.
- Avoid using 'all of the above' as this confuses the student, as they are usually told there is only one answer. It also looks as though the tutor has run out of ideas, so it is probably not the correct answer.
- Avoid negative statements unless highlighted. Having both a negative stem and negative options can be extremely difficult to process.
- Avoid words like 'maybe' and 'usually' as these are difficult to interpret.
- Avoid using words like 'always' and 'never' as students may know the correct answer but feel things can never be that certain.

It is a good idea to select options from common misconceptions that students may have of the topic. Also, develop MCQs with a colleague, as they are very difficult to do well on your own.

✎ ACTIVITY 5B

What's wrong with these MCQs?

Check the list of dos and don'ts above when writing MCQs. Can you recognize some of the problems below?

1. A group of islands is called an:
   (a) peninsula
   (b) archipelago
   (c) moraine
   (d) polder

2. In education, which one of the following publications is considered to be a prime source for research articles:
   (a) *Journal of Educational Psychology*
   (b) *Journal of Educational Measurement*
   (c) *Journal of Clinical Psychology*
   (d) *Review of Educational Research*

3. How many permutations are possible in a bridge hand?

4. If planned aggregate expenditure is greater than national income and the short-run aggregate supply curve is horizontal, the economy:
   (a) Cannot be on the aggregate demand curve.
   (b) Cannot be on the short-run aggregate supply curve.
   (c) Cannot be on the long-run aggregate supply curve.
   (d) Both (b) and (c) are correct.

(These examples were taken from the Castle project Web site at Leicester University.)

Answers

1. The question ends with 'an', suggesting that the next word must start with a vowel.

2. Answer (d), which is correct, is the only one that has the word 'research' in it, which matches the word in the question. Either they all should have the word 'research' or none of them.

3. If you don't play bridge you can't answer this question, and if it is not testing your bridge playing abilities, it can't be considered fair.

4. Answer (d) is very confusing as students usually assume in these tests that only one answer is correct. Also, this kind of answer suggests a tutor who has run out of ideas.

MCQs and learning outcomes

Most learning outcomes, in terms of cognitive skills, can be written from Bloom's *cognitive domain* taxonomy (see 5.2.1 above). We can also use this when writing MCQs, although this is not a 'black and white' science.

1. *Cognitive domain: knowledge*

Stem	Who wrote 'Mein Kampf?
Options	a. Weber
	b. Hitler
	c. Engels
	d. Marx
Comments	Note: all options are consistent and have German names. The question is testing the students' ability to recall facts.

2. *Cognitive domain: comprehension*

Stem	Which one of the following describes what takes place in the so-called *preparation* stage of the creative process, as applied to the solution of a particular problem?
Options	a. The problem is identified and defined.
	b. All available information about the problem is collected.
	c. An attempt is made to see if the proposed solution to the problem is acceptable.
	d. The person goes through some experience leading to a general idea of how the problem can be solved.
	e. The person sets the problem aside, and gets involved with some other unrelated activity.
Comments	The student needs to be able to recall information about the creative process, and understand the various stages in order to identify the one being tested. (Castle Project, 1998)

3. *Cognitive domain: application*

Stem	Jeff, wife Karen, and son Mike sit down to dinner. Watch what takes place on the video clip and then choose the most appropriate description from the list below.
Option	a. The son has a rebellious attitude and needs to be disciplined.
	b. The father vented his frustration on his son and failed to identify the root problem.
	c. The wife undermined her husband's authority and has sided with her son.
Comments	This is an example of a multimedia MCQ where a small video clip is used. The students are being tested on their application of learnt information/ theories in a new or practical situation. A set of options could be offered where students determine the most appropriate analysis of the video clip within a given theory.

4. *Cognitive domain: analysis*

Stem 1	Alice, Barbara and Charles own a small business: the Chock-Full-o-Goodness Cookie Company. Because Charles has many outside commitments and Barbara has a few, Alice tends to be most in touch with the daily operations of the company. As a result, when financial decisions come down to a vote at their monthly meeting, they have decided that Alice gets eight votes, Barbara gets seven, and Charles gets two – with nine being required to make the decision. According to the *minimum-resource coalition* theory, who is most likely to be courted for their vote?
Option 1	a. Alice
	b. Barbara
	c. Charles
	d. No trend towards any specific person.
Stem 2	Using the scenario above, who is the most likely to be courted for their vote according to the *minimum-power coalition* theory?
Option 2	a. Alice
	b. Barbara
	c. Charles
	d. No trend towards any specific person.
Comments	This is testing the application of the two theories for a given scenario. Students need to differentiate between the theories. (Georgeanne Cooper and Michael Sweet, 1999, University of Oregon)

5. *Cognitive domain: synthesis*

Stem	The following is a study of the effects of lecturers' support on psychology test performance. On the first day they performed a psychology test during which they were provided with assistance from a lecturer. On the second day the same subjects performed the same test, but without the assistance of a lecturer. The number of correct answers on the test was the dependent variable (DV); whether lecturer support was provided or not was the independent variable (IV). Which of the following would you say is the main problem with the design of the study as presented here?
Option	a. It does not use a standard psychological test.
	b. It does not control for possible carry-over effects from one condition to the second.
	c. It will not produce interval data, therefore powerful parametric statistical tests cannot be performed.
	d. The IV is not varied by the researcher, therefore causal statements cannot be made. (Dr John Everatt, University of Surrey)
Comments	Analysis, synthesis and evaluation can be tricky to hold apart under the Bloom taxonomy. Some may argue this belongs to analysis, which would be a fair comment. It could be argued here that the students are being tested on their ability to creatively apply the statistical knowledge they have learnt.

You could use hybrid tests where MCQs are used by the students to select the correct answer, but then they have to support it with evidence. Marking is twofold: on the correct answer (objective) and then on supporting evidence. You have to decide how to mark if the supporting evidence shows no sign of understanding the question correctly.

For the software used in producing MCQs, see the Active*Guide.

Uses for MCQs

Multiple-choice questions or quizzes can have several functions. The most obvious is to test how well a student is doing. This could form part of a summative assessment. One of the arguments for using MCQs as summative assessment is that such tests can cover the whole course so that students need to have a broad understanding of the issues raised. The essay, on the other hand, will cover one or two topics within the course, but in more detail. You need to decide which is better for your course and students.

MCQs can be used as a diagnostic tool during a course to see how everyone is doing. The tests can be tutor marked and then adjustments made to activities to take into account how well the material is being learnt. They can also be used as a diagnostic tool in an open learning environment. The tests need to be furnished with good feedback, enabling students to see where they went wrong and where they can go to get the appropriate information for revision.

Mini MCQ tests can be used during lectures. You can put up three or four questions at the beginning of the lecture – possibly on an OHP. Students can be expected to answer them or simply reflect on them. At the end of the lecture they try the questions again, and if they cannot answer them, some remedial work needs doing. An alternative version of this is to put the questions on the Web site prior to the lectures, with students expected to have given the questions some thought.

MCQs are a very important part of tutorial material – especially online tutorials. In this case it is better to provide automatic feedback/answers so students can adjust their own studies. If you cannot manage automated feedback, you could provide a simple link to the answer page with feedback. In these instances you are not concerned if students 'cheat': this is part of their learning and not a summative assessment.

The Castle Project (Computer Assisted Teaching and Learning)

http://www.le.ac.uk/cc/ltg/castle/

The CASTLE toolkit has been developed so that tutors and course managers can create online interactive MCQs quickly and easily without any prior knowledge of HTML, cgi, or similar scripting languages. The CASTLE Project was funded by JISC/JTAP.

The Implementation and Evaluation of Computer Assisted Assessment Project (TLTP Phase 3)

http://www.lboro.ac.uk/departments/dis/cti/infocus8/caa.htm

This project aims to produce models that can be used by individuals (good practice) and institutions (strategic issues) to implement and evaluate CAA. They will also be producing training materials and evaluating the cost-effectiveness of different types of CAA.

Writing Multiple-choice Questions that Demand Critical Thinking

Georgeanne Cooper and Michael Sweet (1999), University of Oregon

http://darkwing.uoregon.edu/~tep/assessment/mc4critthink.html

This is part of their Teaching Effectiveness Program. An interesting site that contains the following sections: Important Considerations, Bloom's Taxonomy of Cognitive Levels, Practical Suggestions for Writing Exams, Techniques for Creating Questions, and a Bibliography.

5.3.2   Assessing collaborative learning events

Collaborative learning personalizes knowledge through social activity and emphasizes cooperative efforts along with content-specific knowledge.

Pedagogically it is student-centred, cooperative (rather than individualistic and competitive), tutor-managed from a distance and is ideal for problem solving, analysis and discussion. Researchers have found that collaborative learning develops the higher levels skills of Bloom's taxonomy: analysing, synthesizing, evaluating and conceptualizing (Kimber, 1994).

Collaborative learning can come in many guises, from mini assignments where it is essentially a joint effort on an exercise, to research-centred projects where some form of project management must be established in order to complete the project. It is important, however, to prepare students for collaborative learning and ensure they know what to expect during the process and what the criteria of the final product are. Starting with mini assignments may be a good introduction.

In addition, if collaborative learning is to be taken seriously by students, then the assessment procedures need to be congruent with the learning activities. If the assessment is totally focused on the 'end product', there will be very little reflection on the collaborative process itself.

In this section we will discuss a sample of learning events: problem-based/case-based learning, and online discussion groups as a sample.

Assessing problem-based/case-based learning

Collaborative learning events such as problem-based and case-based learning scenarios comprise both a *product*, which is the main purpose of the group activity, and a *process* of arriving at the final product. Both aspects need to be assessed.

Assessing the product

This is very particular to the kind of group project the students are working on. Clarify with students what is being achieved (learning outcomes) in terms of:

- content;
- cognitive skills – check out Bloom's taxonomy from the cognitive domain, see section 5.2.1;

- procedural/professional skills – what key skills are being developed through the project that affect the end product?

Deciding how to grade the group product can also be difficult. Jolly (1997) made an agreement with her students that if the product were graded at 75 per cent, for example, then each member of the group received that grade. A group contract was established at the beginning stating that all would receive one grade. However, if someone broke that contract and did not contribute equally, then the group had the right to sanction that person, agreeing what percentage of work they had produced and receiving the appropriate grade. This is a safeguard for those responsible students.

Assessing the process

This is an ideal scenario for assessing the effectiveness of students' ability to work as a team. You may want to develop a proforma that will allow students to reflect on their team skills; an example is given in Figure 5.3.

Reflections on Teamwork

Name: _____

Project: _____ **Date** _____

Commented on by: _____

Roles

Include areas of responsibility within the group with/without names.
How did you arrive at areas of responsibility?
General comments on how effective the roles were.

What would you do differently next time?

Handling meetings

Were roles assigned for meetings?
Comments on working through the stages of team development.
How were meetings structured: Agenda? Chairperson? Minute-taker? Was this
 structure discussed beforehand, or did it develop?
How focused was the group?
How were the group interactions in terms of the goals set for meetings?

What would you do differently next time?

Following through decisions

Were the actions of meetings clear?
Did members of the group fulfil their tasks effectively?
Were there any problems getting the group to work together?

What would you do differently next time?

Comments from another group member

Did you see the team in the same way?

Figure 5.3 *Proforma for reflecting on teamwork*

This should not be a lengthy document and the italic print in Figure 5.3 is merely a prompt. It is helpful for students to have their reflections read by another member of the group. Comments on how differently they saw the group would be interesting. There should be a maximum of two A4 pages for this exercise. To carry out this reflective process, students would need to keep a journal of activities that took place during the teamwork and from that produce their reflective report.

Don't forget that teamwork is one of the major key skills that students in higher education need to develop, so if this can be embedded in the course correctly, the model can be used time and time again. Students should be encouraged to keep their reflective documents so that they can build effectively on their skills. This then offers progression through the skill.

Using technology

Technology can be used in both the product and process aspects of the group work. The product may comprise a CAD drawing, a spreadsheet, Web pages, an exhibition, an electronic portfolio or a computer teaching package, to name but a few examples. Students would need to be familiar with the chosen technology and you would need to be able to view their end product. If you expect students to use a certain piece of software, it is advisable that they are trained in its use and that computers are flexibly accessible for this (see section 2.2).

With regard to the process, electronic communication can be used as a method of evidencing the meeting activities of the group. The groups can meet face-to-face and record their agendas and minutes electronically along with any other documentation they develop as part of the process. If face-to-face meetings are not viable (especially for part-time students) then online groups can be established for much of the collaborative work. They will, however, need to meet face-to-face at critical points in the project. You and the group will need to decide if you have ongoing access to these discussions (as an observer), or whether the record of the discussions (archived on to a Web page) will be sufficient for assessment purposes.

Once again you will need to set criteria for assessing these discussions. You might want to consider how efficient they were in the roles assigned to them as evidenced by the online discussions.

✎ ACTIVITY 5C

What assessment criteria would you set for the 'reflections on teamwork' document?

Develop three criteria that you could use to assess the quality of such a report. What would the learning outcome be for completing this kind of report?

Checklist

- Discuss the whole process fully with your students before starting.
- Make the areas of assessment clear. Are you prepared to negotiate any of the assessment criteria?

- Do you want to include peer assessment? If so, how will you incorporate it?
- You will need assessment criteria for:
  – the end product;
  – the reflective documentation of the process;
  – any use of online discussion material in support of the project.

Create Your Own Electronic Portfolio (using off-the-shelf software)

Dr Helen Barrett (1999) University of Alaska

http://transition.alaska.edu/www/portfolios/toolsarticle.html

Helen Barrett has written a wide selection of articles on this topic, and from this article you can move to others. This article looks at how existing software can be used to create electronic portfolios: databases, hypermedia 'card' software, multimedia authoring packages, the Web, Adobe Acrobat, and multimedia slide shows such as Microsoft PowerPoint and video (both digital and analogue). We are seeing an increasing interest in portfolios that are generally used with independent learning where students are given a set of learning outcomes, tuition and resources. They then produce a portfolio that evidences how they achieved those learning outcomes. Portfolios can be produced by the individual or a group. You will need to set up criteria once again in marking the portfolios.

Electronic Portfolios in Higher Education: Their value for faculty, students and employers

Dr Marsha Leeman-Conley (1998) National University Sacramento

http://www.softcom.net/users/conley/papers/ICIE98.html

The contents of this article are: what is an electronic portfolio, what is the purpose of a portfolio, how will students learn to develop their portfolio, what format should the portfolio have, an example of an MBA portfolio. This is a good 'all-round' article to get you into the topic.

Assessing online discussions

An example of this kind of activity is the online seminar or conference. Buckner and Morss (1998) used online seminars effectively with a fairly structured approach. They had several 'conferences' running and participants (approximately 13 per group) were assigned a role as either conference leader or contributor. Each conference ran for one week. The conference leader was required to make an opening statement of 500 words (with appropriate references) and be proactive in the discussion. Contributors to the conferences were expected to make two contributions taking into account the opening statement and contributions of other participants, as well as incorporating other evidence and reflecting on their own experience. In all, contributors took part in three other conferences. The conference leader ended the discussion with a 500-word closing statement.

Marks were awarded to individuals for their contributions and comprised 33 per cent of the module. The paper does not reveal the assessment criteria used, but students were graded according to their ability to both lead and contribute to the debate. They also carried out an online problem-solving activity, which they thought less successful as they found it difficult to make decisions at a distance.

Using the technology

Generally speaking, the kinds of technology you can use for online discussions are:

- e-mail;
- mailing lists, eg Majordomo;
- conferencing – see section 4.5.5.

When deciding which technology to use, it is important to be able to easily assess individual contributions. You want to be able to group contributions by name, topic and date. You can either assess the range of contributions of an individual, or how a particular topic was developed and by whom. What will the criteria be?

Make sure you:

- Discuss the whole process with your students before you start.
- Decide how you are going to set up your discussion group – the management of it.
- Decide how you will assess the contributions of individuals.
- Develop assessment criteria and discuss them with students.
- Decide the kind of technology best suited to this, given your institutional constraints of course – check the Active*Guide.
- Make sure your students know how to use the technology and understand their roles and function within the group.
- If you are setting a time limit, make sure there is flexible access to PCs during this time.
- Make sure you know how to access the data you need for the assessment.

 ## ACTIVITY 5D

Developing criteria for assessing online contributions

Consider the online discussion conferencing example of Buckner and Morss. What criteria would you use to assess individual contributions in an electronic environment?

5.4   Automating and managing assessment

Section 5.3.1 lists the types of objective test questions that are possible using CAA and provides advice on creating effective non-trivial questions. This section looks at the technologies that are available to automate the delivery and marking of objective tests and describes how they are used in practice.

5.4.1 Optical Mark Reading: OMR

Not all assessment technologies require students to have access to a computer. It is possible to automatically process printed multiple-choice tests and questionnaires using a scanner and suitable software – this is known as optical mark reading (OMR). Note that only multiple-choice questions can be set, since the software cannot understand handwritten answers.

The test forms can be designed using any word-processor or desktop publishing (DTP) program, provided a few guidelines are followed, and laser-printed or photocopied as required. There is no need for the specially printed paper with punched registration holes that were required by older technologies. The students indicate their answers by 'filling in' the appropriate circle on the test form. An example of an OMR-assessed question is shown in Figure 5.4.

Q1	The Moon stays in orbit around the Earth due to the action of which of these forces? *select all that apply*	gravity	○
		centrifugal force	●
		centipetal force	●
		gyroscopic force	○
		angular momentum	○

Figure 5.4 *An example of a question assessed using OMR software*

The OMR software uses modern optical character recognition (OCR) techniques to work out which answers are marked on each test form and stores all the results in a file. The use of a scanner with an automatic sheet-feeder is essential to make the process efficient, otherwise someone will have to manually scan every form – a very laborious and dull process. If the forms are folded or creased, it will be necessary to photocopy them before scanning to avoid paper jams.

Most OMR software is able to process the answers to produce simple statistics and charts that show the distribution of marks, average scores and standard deviation. More complex analysis is possible by importing the results file into a spreadsheet or specialized statistics program.

There are problems in identifying which test form belongs to which student. In order to match the student to the work, you have to assign each student a unique code that can be read by the OMR software. Students must mark this code at the top of every form they complete. If this technology is adopted, it may be a good idea to make sure students use the same code for every test they take. An example of coding student identity is shown in Figure 5.5.

Course evaluation questionnaires avoid this problem of identity since they are usually anonymous. Using OCR can minimize the amount of laborious work involved in collating and processing the results to produce the quantitative analysis required by many institutional quality assurance procedures. The qualitative data is much harder to capture using OMR since it cannot 'read' hand-written answers. This is unhelpful, since the students' answers to questions like, 'How would you improve this course?' are probably of greater

Please mark your student code *(AED in this example)*										
Code letter	**A**	**B**	**C**	**D**	**E**	**F**	**G**	**H**	**I**	**J**
1st letter:	●	○	○	○	○	○	○	○	○	○
2nd letter:	○	○	○	○	●	○	○	○	○	○
3rd letter:	○	○	○	●	○	○	○	○	○	○

Figure 5.5   *An example of coding student identity for OMR software*

value to you in thinking about future changes than in knowing that you scored an average of 3.7 on 'How do you rate the teaching?' See the Active*Guide for one solution to this problem, but note that it is dependent on specific OMR software.

Overall, OMR technology has the advantage that you can continue to use paper-based tests and questionnaires, but this has to be weighed against its limitations and the greatly superior capabilities and efficiency of CAA.

5.4.2   CAA for summative and formative assessment

Let's start by thinking about what it might be like to use CAA for a summative test.

At the end of a lecture you remind your students that there will be a test the following week that contributes 20 per cent towards their grade for that module. You tell them the date, time and location of the test. Inconveniently, you have had to book three computer rooms in order to accommodate the whole class, and this has meant organizing three teaching assistants to invigilate the test and assist the students. Since the computer rooms are not very close together, you need to divide the class into three groups and assign each group to a specific room, otherwise there is bound to be last-minute confusion.

On the day of the test the students go to the appropriate computer room and access the course's Web site. This has a brief introduction to the test and a link to the test itself. They start by entering their unique username and password so that the CAA system can identify them. Each student can start when ready, since the system will time them individually.

They work through the test by making multiple-choice selections, typing in single-word answers, and entering their answers to calculations. The CAA system uses Web-based forms to record the answers entered by each student. At the end of the allotted time the system will not accept further answers and the test is over. The teaching assistants have been wandering around, providing assistance if appropriate but mostly ensuring there is no collaboration between students or reference to Web pages. For an example of how these questions might look on screen, see Figure 5.6.

After the tests are completed, the CAA system will automatically mark them and store the results. It will also automatically collate and analyse the results so you can easily see the results for the whole class, for each student and for each question. The latter

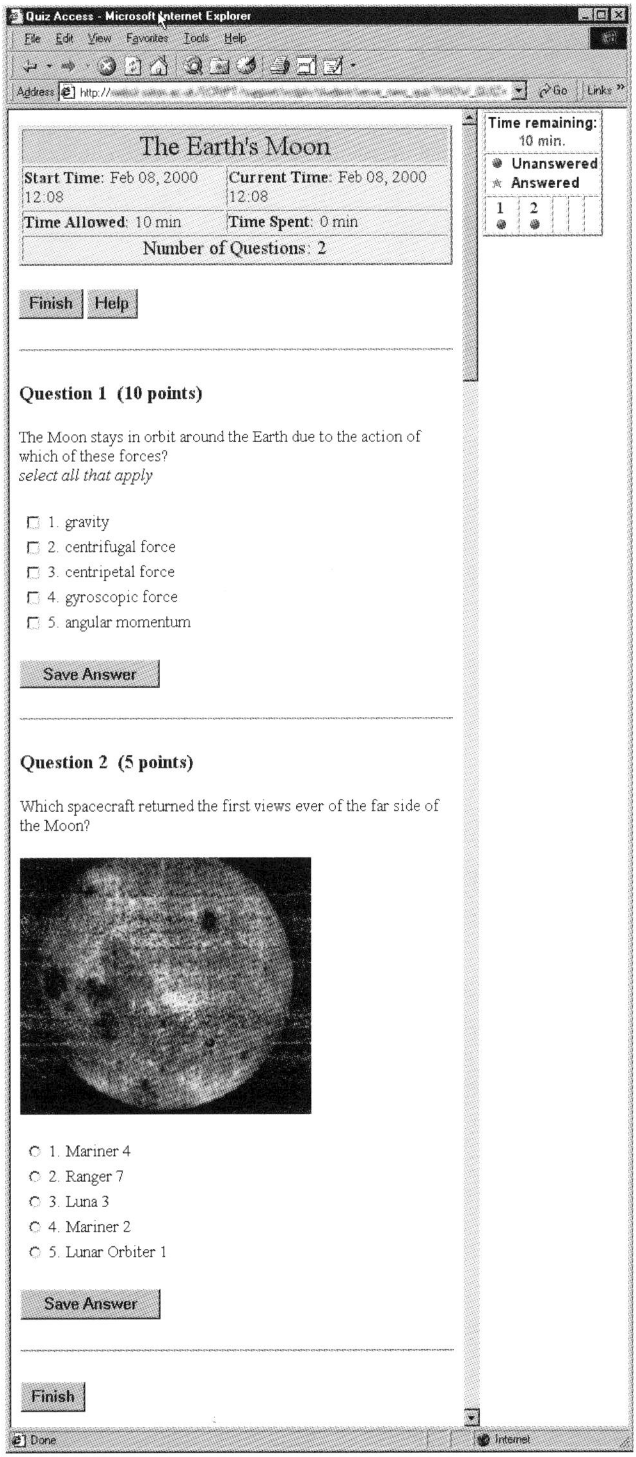
Quiz Access - Microsoft Internet Explorer
File Edit View Favorites Tools Help
Address http://
Go Links
The Earth's Moon
Start Time: Feb 08, 2000 12:08
Current Time: Feb 08, 2000 12:08
Time Allowed: 10 min
Time Spent: 0 min
Number of Questions: 2
Finish Help
Question 1 (10 points)
The Moon stays in orbit around the Earth due to the action of which of these forces?
select all that apply
1. gravity
2. centrifugal force
3. centripetal force
4. gyroscopic force
5. angular momentum
Save Answer
Question 2 (5 points)
Which spacecraft returned the first views ever of the far side of the Moon?
1. Mariner 4
2. Ranger 7
3. Luna 3
4. Mariner 2
5. Lunar Orbiter 1
Save Answer
Finish
Time remaining: 10 min.
Unanswered
Answered
1 2
Done
Internet

Figure 5.6

will give you valuable feedback on how well you are teaching (and the students are learning) that part of the syllabus.

A couple of days later you release the results to the students so that when they access the CAA system using their username and password they can see their marks, as well as feedback on their answers, which includes suggestions for remedial study where appropriate. As a final step, you de-restrict the test so that the students can use it as a revision aid before the end-of-year exam.

Now that we've seen the overall process, let's look at some of the detail.

Creating the test questions

Earlier sections in this chapter have discussed how to write effective, fair and pedagogically sound questions. Entering those questions plus their answers, marks and feedback into a CAA system is easy by comparison, but is a very laborious task which requires a methodical approach and good quality control. Most tutors write all the questions, answers and feedback in a word-processor and then cut-and-paste them to the CAA system one small chunk at a time, double-checking everything before progressing to the next question. This investment in time and effort will be repaid by the automated marking and data analysis, provided the test can be used more than once with sufficiently large groups of students.

It is possible to use CAA systems to automate the course evaluation questionnaires required each year for every course taken by every student. Most academics and departments regard these as a thankless chore, despite the valuable feedback they provide. Some systems can even differentiate between tests and surveys and automatically make the survey data anonymous. You can tell who has and who has not completed the survey, but you don't know who made each response.

Most CAA systems support 'pools' of questions that can be used to create individualized tests. For example, you might create four pools of 10 questions each to cover four topics. Each student would get a test containing three questions from each pool, chosen at random. Provided all the questions in a pool are equivalent in terms of difficulty and marks, this is an excellent way to minimize collusion between students. It also makes possible repeated use of the test as a learning tool.

Some subject areas are developing large banks of questions that can be freely used. This is obviously much more efficient than writing all your own questions, since you can select those that match your courses. The CAA Centre and the new Learning and Teaching Support Network subject centres will be able to advise you if question banks exist that match your needs.

Computer Assisted Assessment Centre

http://caacentre.ac.uk

This national HEFCE-funded centre has a great deal of further information and resources, including links to subject-specific questions sets, CAA software, research papers, how-to guides, Web sites and books.

📖 **Learning Technology Support Network (LTSN)**

http://www.ltsn.ac.uk/

This new network of subject centres will provide links to relevant resources and case studies. There is also a 'generic centre' to support the use of C&IT generally, including CAA.

Some CAA systems can import suitably coded text directly to create question pools. The codes indicate whether a piece of text is a question, an answer, its mark or its feedback, and rely on a defined structure for each question. It may be possible to automatically process question banks to add the codes used by your CAA system using some simple programming. An example of a coded question is shown in Figure 5.7.

```
# QUESTION 1 - anything preceded by a hash mark is a comment
:TYPE:MC:1
:TITLE:moon orbit
:CAT:forces
:QUESTION
The Moon stays in orbit around the Earth due to the action of which of
these forces?<BR><I>select all that apply</I>
# these are the answers, with percentage marks for each
:ANSWER1:20:H
gravity
:ANSWER2:30:H
centrifugal force
:ANSWER3:30:H
centripetal force
:ANSWER4:0:H
gyroscopic force
:ANSWER5:20:H
angular momentum
# this is the feedback to the answers
:REASON1
correct - gravity pulls the Moon and the Earth together, but what force
counteracts this and keeps the Moon in orbit?
...REASON2
correct - the angular momentum of the Moon as it orbits the Earth exerts a
centrifugal force that counters the gravitational force
...REASON3
correct - gravity exerts a centripetal force that pulls the Moon and the
Earth together and is countered by the centrifugal force
:REASON4
incorrect - gyroscopic force plays no part in maintaining the Moon's orbit
:REASON5
correct - the angular momentum of the Moon as it orbits the Earth exerts a
centrifugal force that counters the gravitational force
```

Figure 5.7 *Example of a question coded for use in tests delivered using WebCT*

Delivering the test

The first problem is often getting access to enough computers so that every student takes the test at the same time. This will always be the case for summative tests, although formative tests can be more flexible with the timing. For example, some CAA systems can be set to allow the test to be taken at any time between two defined dates and times, with the responsibility on individual students to find a suitable computer and do so. Multiple attempts at a test may also be allowed, with the aim of helping the students to learn, although randomized tests based on question banks will increase the value of this approach.

If more than one computer room is needed to accommodate the students, additional administration is needed to assign them to a particular room. This is especially important if the rooms are some distance apart, as is often the case. Teaching assistants will be required to invigilate the tests and be capable of providing simple technical support if needed.

Invigilation is a real problem with networked computers. It is easy to use programs such as Web browsers to access information illicitly or even use Internet 'chat' software to confer with other students in the room or elsewhere. Invigilators will need to be aware of the potential methods and prowl the room constantly to stand any chance of detecting such cheating. Alternatively, it may be possible to implement technical restrictions temporarily on the network to disable access to the Web.

Reliability is also an issue, since students will certainly complain if technical problems affect them. These range from slow network connections, through program crashes, to server problems or network failures. A policy for dealing with these needs to be thought through in advance. It is inconvenient if the problem means that the students are unable to take the test, but potentially disastrous if things go wrong during the test.

One point worth mentioning is that one of the worst things you can do is to have every student try to access the test at the same moment by saying, 'You can start the test... *now.*' They all click the link to the test simultaneously and the server is overwhelmed and responds very slowly. It is much better to phase the start and let the CAA system ensure everyone gets the same length of time – a simple technique is for the invigilator to walk round the room and students start as he or she passes by.

Marking

CAA systems often provide sophisticated marking options that extend the possibilities of the multiple-choice test format. For example, different marks can be assigned to specific answers, avoiding the simplistic 'right or wrong' approach. These marks can be negative to discourage guessing or penalize ignorance of essential topics. The challenge is to use this flexibility to develop a marking scheme that is fair and able to differentiate effectively students with varying levels of understanding and knowledge.

You will also need to think carefully about the feedback you provide to each question. Should it give the right answer, say why the answer was right or wrong, or provide hints to help the student find the right answer? In a Web-based system, these hints might include live links to relevant resources.

Many CAA systems allow questions that require the student to type a paragraph or so. They are unable to mark these automatically (yet!) but will allow you to access the answers and manually enter a mark for them. Some systems enable you to let your teaching assistants log on to the system and share this task.

The test result and feedback are potentially available to the students as soon as they have submitted the test, unless some questions require manual marking as described above. However, you may wish to delay releasing the results until you have had a chance to look at them. Most systems will automatically provide a detailed analysis of both the overall results and individual questions, neatly avoiding a good deal of tedious data entry and spreadsheet work.

There is a trend towards CAA systems that can be integrated into institutional administration systems, so that test results are automatically stored with each student's central record of achievement and can be used to calculate final grades. This is still rare at present, but is a sign of the growing commercialization of the education industry.

ACTIVITY 5E
Checklist for Chapter 5

1. Determine the aims of your course or unit.
2. What level is it?
3. How many learning hours do you estimate for this course?
4. Of the learning hours, how many are:
   - contact hours with the tutor;
   - independent learning;
   - collaborative learning?
5. What are the learning outcomes for the course? Check section 5.2.1 – do your learning outcomes need to be balanced across the cognitive, affective and psychomotor domains? How balanced are they within the cognitive domain?
6. Are these learning outcomes in line with (map onto) the student programme as a whole?
7. What teaching and learning strategies can you use to facilitate these learning outcomes?
8. What formative and summative assessment procedures will you use?
9. If you are thinking of using technology, will:
   - students be using technology to complete the assessment, eg a multimedia essay;
   - you use it to deliver the assessment;
   - you use it to mark MCQ tests?

   How much time do you estimate to set this up and get the necessary training? Do you know where you can get help?

References

Bloom, B and Krathwohl, D (1956) *Taxonomy of Educational Objectives: The classification of educational goals. Handbook I: Cognitive domain*, Longmans, New York

Buckner, K and Morss, K (1998) 'The importance of task appropriateness in computer-supported collaborative learning', *Alt-J*, **7** (1), pp 33–8

Educational Testing Service Network, Higher Education Assessment, http://www.ets.org/hea/heaweb.html

Hinett, K and Thomas, J (eds) (1999) *Staff Guide to Self and Peer Assessment*, The Oxford Centre for Staff and Learning Development, Oxford

Hounsell, D, McCulloch, M and Scott, M (1996) *The ASSHE Inventory: Changing assessment practices in Scottish higher education*, UCOSDA, Sheffield

Jolly, L (1997) 'Reflexive journals', http://mama.minmet.uq.edu.au/~radcliff/surfer/reflex.htm

Kimber, D (1994) 'Collaborative learning in management education: issues, benefits, problems and solutions: a literature review', http://ultibase.eu.rmit.edu.au/Articles/kimbe1.html

Krathwohl, D, Bloom, B and Masia, B (1964) *Taxonomy of Educational Objectives: The classification of educational goals. Handbook II: Affective domain*, David McKay Co, New York

Ramsden, P (1994) 'Using research on student learning to enhance educational quality', published by DeLiberations, http://www.lgu.ac.uk/deliberations/ocsd-pubs/isltp-ramsden.html

Mowl, G, McDowell, L and Brown, S (1996) 'What is innovative assessment?', published by DeLiberations, http://www.lgu.ac.uk/deliberations/assessment/mowl_content.html

Walklin, L (1991) *The Assessment of Performance and Competence: A handbook for teachers and trainers*, Stanley Thorne, Cheltenham

6 Concluding comments

The estimated set-up cost of the UK *e-university* project, announced in February 2000 by the government (*Times Higher Education Supplement*, 18 February 2000), is £200 million over two years. Half of the funds for this are coming from the government and the other half from the private sector, such as telecommunications and publishing industries. These education–commerce links, forming new kinds of universities, are now happening across the globe with the aim of delivering online distance courses.

C&IT in education, however, is not restricted to these flagship projects. Students themselves are coming through the education system with expectations that include the use of technology for accessing resources and communicating. We are seeing this already at primary and secondary school level, where the use of C&IT is set to increase. Outside school, children are able to get online support for the National Curriculum, homework clubs and careers via, for example, BBC online services and the DfEE's Connexions Web site. Likewise, teachers in schools are increasingly served by the National Grid for Learning. Technology, through both school and home entertainment, is becoming an integral part of our lives and tertiary education must fully embrace this.

In HE and FE, academic tutors are now not only faced with learning how to apply these technologies to their teaching craft, but also how they can be applied within an educational framework that encourages autonomous learning and supports collaborative work. This kind of learning environment relies on students *reflecting* on their own progression through their learning – so we are seeing an increase in 'reflective logs' that give students a framework to do this. Tutors are also encouraged to take on this reflective approach within their teaching. Indeed, the membership application form for the recently established UK professional body for teaching in higher education, the Institute for Learning and Teaching (ILT), specifically asks applicants to reflect on a wide range of their teaching skills. Good reflective skills are essential for successful autonomous or independent learning, be they learners or academic tutors.

Autonomous learning, which has always been to varying degrees part of university life, has a new impetus with C&IT. Communications technologies allow learning communities to develop distance and open learning, while the Web and CD ROMs allow us to produce integrated learning environments housing a wide variety of learning resources, from primary, experiential to pedagogically structured material. Our task now is to learn how to exploit the possibilities of these technologies to the full, both pedagogically and technically.

In order to achieve this, we need to understand how we can produce (or buy) digital multimedia resources, the software needed to deliver these and how they can be incorporated pedagogically to produce a cohesive learning environment. This should be an environment that produces activities and assignments coherent with clearly stated learning outcomes, and in which students understand the criteria for success.

This also means working within the limitations of our own institutions while being aware of the needs of our students, in terms of their current knowledge in the subject domain, as well as addressing any possible disabilities and lack of skills that might hinder proper access to learning resources.

This book has attempted to synthesize the current situation regarding the need for tertiary educators to embrace these new technologies. There are many Web site links in the book that give you access to a wide variety of further resources. We will be keeping a check on these Web site addresses and will inform you of any changes via the Web site connected with the book – the Active*Guide at http://www.clt.soton.ac.uk/activeguide. In addition, do consult the Active*Guide for up-to-date information on the technology to use, as well as some learning materials to get you started.

Index